BusinessWeek

Preparing Your Business for the Global Economy

McGraw-Hill
New York   San Francisco   Washington, D.C.   Auckland   Bogotá
Caracas   Lisbon   London   Madrid   Mexico City   Milan
Montreal   New Delhi   San Juan   Singapore   Sydney   Tokyo   Toronto

Library of Congress Cataloging-in-Publication Data

Preparing your business for the global economy / BusinessWeek.
      p.   cm.
    Includes index.
    ISBN 0-07-009438-1
    1. Small business—Management.   2. Success in business.
3. Competition, International.   I. Business Week

HD62.7.P725   1997   97-7418
658.02'2—dc21   CIP

McGraw-Hill

*A Division of The **McGraw-Hill** Companies*

Another book from Affinity Communications Corporation
Copyright © 1997 by Affinity Communications Corporation. All rights reserved.
Printed in the United States of America. Except as permitted under the United States
Copyright Act of 1976, no part of this publication may be reproduced or distributed
in any form or by any means, or stored in a database or retrieval system, without the
prior written permission of the publisher.

1 2 3 4 5 6 7 8 9 0   DOW/DOW   9 0 2 1 0 9 8 7

ISBN 0-07-009438-1

McGraw-Hill books are available at special quantity discounts to use as premiums and sales
promotions or for use in corporate training programs. For more information, please write to
the Director of Special Sales, McGraw-Hill, 11 West 19th Street, New York, NY 10011, or
contact your local bookstore.

Printed and bound by R. R. Donnelley and Sons, Inc.

 This book is printed on recycled, acid-free paper containing a minimum of 50% recycled, de-inked fiber.

Designer: Janet Brandt
Developmental Editors: Mari Florence and Melinda Gordon, backbone books
Photographs: PhotoDisk™

Table of Contents

Introduction

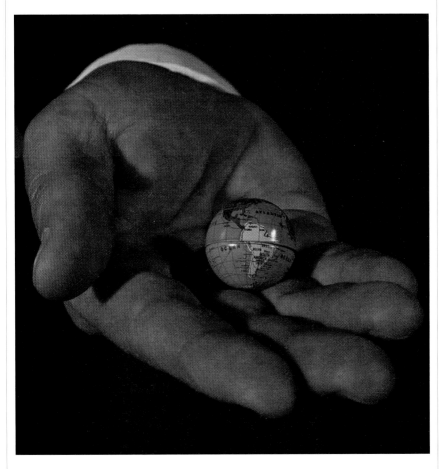

An old Chinese proverb tells of two lovers separated by endless distances of land and countless stretches of sea. The forlorn boy calls out that if only he could shrink the land and the seas, he could again meet his sweetheart and rekindle the love that was meant to be. Now, if this love-sick lad could have held on for several centuries, he would have seen his wishes come true. Technology and the sudden influx of rapid and easily accessible communications are shrinking the world. Or as anyone with a computer and a modem can at-test, a person's reach has grown dramatically in the last few years.

Evidence abounds that for business purposes, the world is shrinking and undergoing economic unification. Borders are being crossed, fences and walls are falling, and multicultural tolerance is gaining new ground. NAFTA is alive, and as free-trade zones are budding, exporters are drawn by incentives to enter uncharted markets. Asian, Indian, Mexican, and Latin American labor wages remain low (for the near-term). Global labor skills have increased markedly: the Taiwanese have nearly cornered the motherboard manufacturing market, the Israelis are known for their encryption technology, Americans own the global service sector, and Southeast Asia is rapidly becoming the next Detroit. The "virtual world" of computerized and electronic networks is dramatically altering businesses operations, as companies are jumping onto the Internet, subscriptions to the Net increase an average of 10 percent a month, and sites on the World Wide Web continue to multiply. The importance of jobs and free trade has supplanted political differences between countries long known for holding grudges. Another tangible example of global unification, the European Union, is alive and will soon be issuing standardized currency. Localized markets around the world are booming, privatizations are speeding towards the marketplace, and viewing the results of their enterprise, global investors are trumpeting their successes.

And what does all of this mean to you?

Quite a bit, if you're thinking of "going global." In today's worldwide economy, small-business owners and managers are leaping at the prospect of increasing sales by way of entering foreign markets. Entrepreneurs have discovered that foreign markets offer both profit and powerful ancillary benefits, not the least of which is the ability to resuscitate lagging domestic sales. Global trade can counterbalance the "valleys" in the life of a product. Seasonal fluctuations in sales at home could be offset by sales abroad. For scores of products, a shining year of sales abroad can more than make up for a year's listless domestic performance. While a particular North American industry may have reached its peak and start slumping, it may be the hottest thing elsewhere. Rather than shifting to a new industry, many businesses are shifting to new markets. They see the opportunity to do what they do best—albeit overseas—rather than diversify-

ing into another industry where trouble is more often the outcome than profits.

Your company need not be large to enjoy the benefits of this book. Even if you're a sole proprietor, *Preparing Your Business for the Global Economy* will provide valuable information that should help you secure a place within the new economic frontier. You'll learn where the global economy is heading and how you might keep one step ahead of it. And you needn't make a huge initial financial investment to take advantage of the ideas presented here. Even the beginning entrepreneur with an idea and a vision will find this book appealing.

Preparing Your Business for the Global Economy will demonstrate that thinking smartly about markets abroad is quite a bit different than targeting domestic markets. The unique aspects of both a foreign market and the product or service under consideration should be addressed. There's also the question of how to gain familiarity with the trends that characterize the global marketplace. Thereafter, expect a host of factors that do not normally come into play at home, such as language barriers, religious customs, and other logistical considerations; such as, for example, the lack of in-country refrigerated transportation.

To offset some of the barriers and difficulties that are encountered when doing business on a global scale, new and nimble communications technologies have greatly eroded the obstacles posed by borders, geography, and languages. Just a mere handful of countries currently cannot be reached, and access is rapidly expanding. Poised at your phone, fax machine, or—most importantly—your computer console, you will be among millions of people now roaming the planet electronically. IBM predicts that seven hundred million people will be using the Internet by the year 2000, and already, business over the Net is booming. Accordingly, this book details how to conduct your operations along the information super-highway.

The United States government has invested much time and effort into ensuring that American entrepreneurs stepping overseas will not be isolated. The U.S. Department of Commerce (DOC) has set up agencies just to hold your hand. And they are doing a lot of your work for you, too. The DOC continues to work behind the scenes to defuse tensions, preserve cultures, and even promote peace. As a result, and due to the march of Western-style commerce, some of the world's key political tensions are become much more manageable.

Nations are busily becoming allies for economic, not geopolitical, conquest. The stakes are high—daily world trade in goods and services now approaches $12.5 billion. To illustrate the remarkable growth of the global economic infrastructure, consider these statistics: In the space of 10 years, from 1986 to 1996, daily trading in international currency exchanges went from not quite $200 billion to $1.25 trillion—or 100 times the daily volume of the world trade in goods and services. In the U.S. alone, small companies are fueling an export explosion that has more than doubled since 1986 to a total of $696 billion in 1994.

New groups, both within and among countries, are catching on to the importance of economic power. Former friends and foes alike have formed potent new blocs within a more liberalized, innovative trade environment. This environment has been made possible by the General Agreement on Tariffs and Trade (GATT—worldwide), the North American Free Trade Agreement (NAFTA—in North America), and the European Union (EU—in Europe).

Humankind has traded goods and services for centuries and will continue to do so far into the next millennium. It is quite possible, then, that there is a world market for your company's product or service. If you envision a place for your business in the global market, adopt the following goals:

1. Establish a loyal and effective worldwide network of contacts for the distribution and sale of your product or service. Such a network will be the key to your ultimate success.

2. Seek to achieve net profits after no more than a few years' sustained effort. You may find modest near-term success, or you may discover considerable adversity over a substantial period. But after three years, your operation should be profitable in every country you've entered.

Just remember that nothing durable or credible is built in a day. Establishing a profitable foothold takes time, effort, and patience. But there are distributors overseas that exist solely on their ability to push U.S. products. Chapter 1 goes into detail on how to find them and what to look out for.

Once a business owner or manager understands the trends of today's global economy, how does he or she increase profits, whether at home or abroad? Moreover, how does one even enter a foreign market? Is it worth it if the business lacks the confidence to leave the narrow confines of its familiar and comfortable domestic market niches? There are several answers, but the fact is that thousands of existing companies and an untold number of startups have found life, even a good deal of success, by going global.

The following chapters analyze 10 major trends that characterize the quickly unfolding global economy. Included are strategies with which you can begin, enhance, or modify your efforts to tap into foreign territories suitable for your product or service. Also included is advice from businesspeople who have taken their enterprises to a global level, both those who've met with success and those who've been burned. To facilitate with a startup operation, a list of useful contacts is included in the appendix. Finally, a lack of foreign language skills shouldn't necessarily dissuade you. Not all exporters or foreign investors are bi- or multilingual.

In fact, you may find that the book's exploration of the particular "social mindset" of a given foreign market is even more crucial to your business's international success. Management specialist Peter Drucker, emeritus professor of management at the Claremont Business School, agrees that the greatest challenges to global business are social. Regarding Japan, Drucker says that "no one in this country [the U.S.] fully understands the Japanese situation. Yes, there are tremendous barriers in Japan, but they are not economic. They are social."

Once again, *Preparing Your Business for the Global Economy* intends to light the way along the global trail, making the most exotic passage of all—from red ink to black—expeditious and rewarding.

Chapter 1

Small Companies Can Be Powerful Players

I n 1989, RGdata, Inc., a small computer networking company in Rochester, New York, thought it saw overwhelming opportunities in Russia and other former Soviet Bloc countries. Gorbachev's Perestroika was opening up the country, and suddenly the curtain was pulled back on Russia's huge markets. Peeking in—though with a good deal of hesitancy—were corporate Goliaths and small businesses alike.

The business infrastructure Western countries are accustomed to, or at least prefer, was lacking. Shipping to the So-

viet Union was a nightmare and phone communications were worse, not to mention language barriers, cultural differences and a pervasive awareness of the red scare. But the philosophy of RGdata's president, Robert A. Giese, was that if you wait until a market is stable, "everyone will already have a dance partner." So Giese teamed up with three other small companies to pay for a $25,000 booth at a Department of Commerce (DOC)-sponsored trade show in Moscow—and started dancing. By 1994, 20 percent of RGdata's $19 million in business came from former SovietBloc countries. RGdata was a pioneer that could have gone the way of the Twist; but Giese followed his instincts and was rewarded with big profits. Similar and arguably plentiful opportunities exist, enough so that Arthur Anderson and the trade group National Small Business United are studying the matter. They recently conducted a survey of 750 companies with fewer than 500 employees, and results indicated that there is indeed a trend toward a stronger global economy. The study showed that 20 percent of these companies exported products and services in 1994, up from 16 percent in 1993 and 11 percent in 1992. Most experts expect the trend to continue well into the next century, especially as Third World markets are "settled" and grow.

A new global fever is now hitting businesses worldwide, and it's encouraging to note that instead of just benefiting corporate giants, the fever is sweeping through the ranks of small and mid-sized businesses. While growing the marketplace is a business fact of life, a new perspective is shifting the focus on where the growth can occur most successfully. By exporting, smaller firms can escape sluggish sales at home or build on their existing domestic revenues overseas. When the recession of the early 1990s was beating down U.S. construction equipment suppliers, able managers looked abroad and found construction booms in Brazil, Columbia, and Mexico. And tagging along is a whole new stratum of U.S. companies that are looking beyond their bread and butter domestic markets. Among them is a shared perception that new business must be sought elsewhere. The regional or national markets that have long nurtured and sustained these businesses are often mature and do not provide tangible opportunities for growth.

In the '90s and beyond, the smallest companies will be able to master the rules of global commerce. Countries with previously closed markets, or those with shifting and often capricious market policies (China, Thailand, and Russia for instance) are now setting universal and enforced standards for international trade. The rules are becoming easier to understand, and as a result political conflicts and isolated violent clashes are becoming a far rarer occurence (though tribesmen in Indonesia are still throwing spears at Freeport-McMoRan's gold miners). And as it becomes cheaper and more accessible, communications technology will also continue to facilitate foreign exchange.

Companies are just beginning to take advantage of sprouting national and regional agencies that offer both paid services and free or cheap information. Opening foreign markets to U.S. business is a centerpiece of President Clinton's foreign policy. And though the DOC is often accused of being pro-big business, recent years have seen it reaching out more and more to the level of the entrepreneur. Businesses looking for overseas ventures are being aided by programs set up within the DOC and other agencies. Again, this is all part of federal policy. The government wants American business to go overseas and it is there to help. Check the appendix in the back of the book to find one of the government agencies that best suits the needs of your business.

The North American marketplace is no longer big enough for all the goods and services produced domestically, and U.S. businesses will have to start looking overseas for market share. Such is the consensus among many forward-thinking managers and executives. Should you begin to feel the squeeze that has driven so many others abroad, you may find yourself forced to make a similar decision. And once you've decided that your company should go global—and you actually see profitability in broadening your horizons—you'll need to develop a

Companies can protect themselves from local industry recessions by looking into burgeoning global markets.

strategy. Following are several tried and true strategies on global expansion that have been developed by the pioneers.

Identifying Emerging Markets

In our pursuit of knowledge, we read daily of the economic activities in a handful of industrialized countries— whose interest rate just moved a tick, which head-of-state is having dinner with which finance minister, what corporate giant needs to gain ground over a particular corporate behemoth. Even the news that reaches us in regard to emerging markets is often confined to larger countries where recent political consent has given way to more user-friendly borders (Russia, South Africa, Cambodia). More recently, the business media has covered the news of privatizations and burgeoning stock markets. Unfortunately, all the news we read about today is based on older strategy. Those that succeeded are the compa-

nies that made their move several years ago. We're reading about their successes now, but nothing is new here. Entry into a market should be made before market share has already been divided up by other early comers. Without these proactive efforts, there will be no room for the small-business owner. As mentioned earlier, RGdata saw an opportunity early on, and true to the maxim, "first come, first served," the company gained its own foothold abroad.

Looking to the pioneering and often lucrative examples of the first experimenters in newly opened foreign markets, business opportunities are suddenly being sought and found in some of the more exotic areas of the globe. The sweeping changes taking place in political regimes are facilitating this expansion, as governments once at odds are overlooking political and philosophical differences in favor of finding common and economically beneficial footing. This open-mindedness is blossoming by way of open borders and the advent of the information age. Thus, "hot spots" are igniting in localized regions all over the globe. But don't always assume that the entire country is a hot spot. Former McKinsey & Company international consultant Kenichi Ohmae writes that today's "natural business units" are increasingly cities or specific locations or regions in a country rather than the entire country itself. That doesn't mean that you should discount the importance of national and/or political events that may have "sweetened" a particular country. But if you're looking for opportunity, look where local initiative and demand best fit your product or service.

A noteworthy example of a recent, emerging hot spot is Auckland, New Zealand. Revolutionary reforms there have turned the nation into a laboratory of free-market experimentation. Subsidies, prohibitions, and tariffs once used to protect domestic industry have been stripped away, resulting in a resurrection of New Zealand's once lagging economy and dismal trade balances. Gross Domestic Product surged from a

negative in 1991 to 6 percent growth in 1995. Over the same period of time, the country reversed a $1.6 billion deficit into a $1.8 billion surplus. Policies enacted included: the selling-off of state assets (even the telephone monopoly and forestry cutting rights got their walking orders); placing restrictions on collective bargaining (to allow more labor and wage negotiations on a company-by-company basis); abolishing subsidies and import controls; and enacting regulations that require the central bank to prevent annual inflation from rising above 2 percent. Consequently, foreign investors have been infusing capital, and imported products and services have found entry into the country much less difficult.

Another example is Subic Bay, Philippines, the location of the U.S. Navy's largest overseas base until 1992—when it was pushed out to accommodate the launching of a free-trade zone. The very day the troops were being ushered out, the zone

Hot spots such as New Zealand offer expanding opportunities.

officially opened for business. It is now one of the hottest investment sites in Southeast Asia. Since cutting the torturous red tape enshrouding economic activity there, more than $1 billion in foreign investments have been made into the area. More important, Subic allows duty-free imports and a hassle-free export system. "It's really very impressive and as fast as Taiwan," says Kenny Wang, deputy manager of Acer Inc.'s computer plant in there. Should Acer be able to meet its five-year-plan to grow to 19,000 employees from the handful it started with in 1996, Kenny Wang's "fast" prognosis would prove correct. Smaller companies could find space at a 750-acre industrial park a Taiwanese group is developing. And with FedEx's daily flights into and out of a former Navy air-strip, shipping shouldn't be a problem. By attracting so much business to the area, Richard Gordon, the man charged with the task, is now mentioned as a possible candidate for his country's 1998 presidential elections.

Other areas of interest include Oulu, Finland, a remote town of 100,000 people near the arctic circle. Though often locked in darkness, it is the location of Oulu Technopolis, home of the world's best telecommunications and electronics developers. Business forecasters may find it interesting to note that more Finns are wired per capita than Americans.

On the entertainment front, consider Bombay, India, referred to by many as "Bollywood." Bombay's film industry churned out 800 films last year, twice as many as Hollywood. But the redundancy of the locally produced, music-driven melodramas is apparently getting to the public. When dubbed versions of *Jurassic Park* and *Speed* showed up in local theaters, the Indian public dumped the clichéd love stories overwhelmingly in favor of the excitement of resurrected man-eating dinosaurs and runaway city buses. Software and hardware companies like Silicon Graphics Inc., of Mountain View California, are finding unique business opportunities by importing the tools and technology that make it possible to bring slick movies with splashy digital effects to Bombay's huge film market.

With apartheid lifted and a population of up to 4 million (there has never been a census), Soweto, South Africa is poised to become a viable marketplace for foreign products as well. With the recent granting of equality, demographers are predicting that the black majority in South Africa is about to become its largest group of consumers. The business climate is reflecting recent political changes, with an increasing number of blacks filling important and visible law, banking, retail, and accounting positions—positions that were formerly held solely by whites. "You must develop a partnership with the community—and in that, you have protection for your investment," says Max Legodi, executive director of the Soweto Chamber of Commerce. Quick to take the advice was Buildware Market, a recently opened construction supply warehouse. It took on black partners and hired local Sowetans with pickups to deliver its goods rather than maintain its own fleet of trucks. Business has been good for Buildware—locals are perceiving it as part of the community and are turning to it as they would a neighborhood store.

The regions mentioned above are only a few examples of global hot spots. Several others exist, some probably ideal for your company or product. But how do you find them? The answer is research, and by reading on, you'll learn important tips on where to begin.

Important Clues in the Changing Financial Markets

Business schools hammer home the fact that when the value of your country's currency declines steeply in relation to that of another country, your offerings (all else being equal) suddenly become cheaper and more attractive to that particular market. So when the U.S. dollar dropped precipitously against major world currencies in early 1995, Lucerne Farms, a small horsefeed company with 8 employees on the U.S. eastern seaboard, found that its products were 25 percent less expensive in terms of the current value of the Japanese yen than before. That drew an inquiry from a Japanese distributor, and enough orders followed that Lucerne Farms doubled its revenues this year from the $350,000 it had anticipated from U.S. sales. Five new employees have been added, and company president George A. James calls their success "a real shot in the arm." It's important to note, however, that James's experience is not an everyday occurrence. In fact, he was plain lucky to encounter a demand for his product before even searching out a market. Generally, one would be ill-advised to sit around waiting for the phone to ring. Proactive research and networking are still your best bets.

Conversely, the dollar has a habit of rebounding. Those seeking and finding sales overseas must factor such shifts—upturns and downturns in the dollar's strength—into their cost and profitability equations. Keep in mind that a sacrifice in profits may be in order when there is an adverse swing in currency exchange rates. Be prepared to discount your goods and services if you don't want to lose customers to more eager competitors. You're welcome to look toward the day when rates return to those that enabled you to capture those tidy percentage surpluses, but it's risky to build an export business solely on swings in exchange rates.

Instead, your best ammunition for the changing marketplace is a good sense of your product or service's strengths and weaknesses, and the adaptability of your company outside forces. The understanding and willingness to adjust your business strategy when the time calls for it is often the difference between a business that is successful and one that is not.

Keep Your Goods Moving!

You may have heard nightmare stories about value-added taxes, customs paperwork and other unexpected costs incurred when a company looking into foreign expansion conducts a less than thorough due diligence process. Another pitfall to watch out for is a propensity among certain foreign governments to levy discretionary fees on goods and services. If your goods are standing still, you're more likely to be in for an unpleasant surprise than if they are moving. If and when you're nabbed by "hidden" fees, it's best to seek or offer a face-saving compromise for both sides. In 1993, Kerry Ivan, then Chrysler's Southeast Asia director, put 150 Jeeps bound for Phnom Penh in storage in a Bangkok customs warehouse while waiting for hostilities to cease in Cambodia. During the three months the cars spent in the warehouse, customs officials bumped the storage rate from an initial $3 per day per car to a steep $43. The final bill was a whopping $457,000.

Understandably, Ivan almost lost his cool. His first thought was to use the services of a young trade rep, American Michael Dunne, to cajole officials in the Thai Finance Ministry and Board of Investment. Instead, Dunne gave the Chrysler exec a crash course in Asian negotiating style: Be cool. Don't confront. Be persistent. Compromise. Ivan took young Dunne's advice and became a frequent visitor to the Thai Customs Department and the Port Authority himself. After six weeks of daily negotiations, the Thais agreed to knock 30 percent off the bill. Though it may initially be difficult to see the good in a charge that still exceeded $300,000, the episode enabled Chrysler to develop a

The advice of a seasoned trade representative can save you money and help build valuable relationships.

long-term contract and a vital working relationship with the customs authorities and thus was a good for business in the long term.

Should you consider entering Southeast Asia's markets, you might want to take note of a few of trade rep Dunne's tips:

- Study the region's culture, not just the statistics.

- Join up with a trade associate or commerce affiliate from your country.

- Form a team with local affiliates or larger U.S. companies.

- Offer face-saving compromises when problems arise.

- Establish personal relationships through frequent meetings with local executives.

So far, Mike Dunne's own advice has worked well for him. In 1990, with hardly two nickels to rub together, 27-year-old Dunne set off for Thailand.

His brother Tim drove him to the airport and recalls that at the time, he had serious doubts about Mike's sanity: "Did I think he was nuts? Well, yeah." Four years later, Tim joined Mike at his company, Automotive Resources Asia Ltd. (ARA) in Bangkok. With 20 employees, ARA expects $1 million in billings this year—and not all of it will come from companies with billion-dollar purses. Mike figures that as mature markets shrink in the West, there will be room for pioneering small companies and adventurous entrepreneurs in Asian countries as well. "In Asia, the longer your commitment, the greater the dividends, both personal and professional," says the confident Dunne.

Searching for Buyers and Distributors

For 102 years, Bicknell Manufacturing Co. of Rockland, Maine has made industrial drill bits for construction equipment. In the late 1980s, 8 percent yearly growth was a standard, but the 1990 recession caused the construction market to sink, taking with it the demand for Bicknell's products. Riding out the recession was not an answer, and Bicknell began scrambling for new business. "We had to change course," remembers John E. Purcell, Bicknell's general manager. So Bicknell began to explore the opportunities abroad, added Purcell, noting that none of the company's 65 employees had had any foreign experience, and Purcell acknowledges that "there was much trepidation, with a capital T," about entering an unknown marketplace. And yet, because the construction industries in Central and South America were booming while stateside opportunities lagged, Bicknell had to find new markets.

Next came the question of how to access those markets. Like the managers of many modestly sized companies, Purcell sought information from the Small Business Administration and soon attended a SBA-sponsored trade mission in Mexico. While there, he found a distributor for Bicknell's drill bits and since 1993 has been exporting them to Latin America. The company has plans to expand its export business to China and Vietnam next. And their efforts have paid off—by 1995, Bicknell Manufacturing increased international sales by 20 percent over the preceding year. International sales now account for 15 to 20 percent of the company's total revenue.

Trade promotions sponsored by U.S. and state agencies abroad, such as the one attended by Bicknell Manufacturing's John Purcell, draw major players and large crowds. The DOC's Gold Key program has been particularly fruitful for entrepreneurs. It arranges for small-business executives to meet with pre-screened potential partners in foreign countries. Jim DeCarlo, president of the Accident, Maryland-based Phenix Technologies, met his Spanish distributor on such a jaunt. He spent three days in Madrid in 1993, meeting with potential partners at the U.S. embassy. The trip cost the company, which makes electrical equipment, about $3,500—a wise investment, says DeCarlo, who concedes that he "wouldn't have known where to start" to look for a partner. DeCarlo also recently lined up a $400,000 revolving credit line for his export business with the help of a guarantee from the Maryland Industrial Development Financing Authority.

There are still caveats. While government agencies are eager to help, be aware of the "word on the street" by researching the organizations, or—better yet—speaking to managers at other companies about their experiences with a particular agency or program. These offerings are often poorly funded, even though the SBA and the Export-Import Bank have recently doubled the size of their financing programs.

Some small-business owners, without benefit of government programs, allot as much as a third of their time to globe-trotting in order to network with potential clients and drum up business. Entrepreneur Katherine Allen has made contacts from Singapore to Sao Paulo based on this approach, and figures that fully half of her yearly $4 million in sales comes from exports. After two years of travel and numerous meetings, Chinese customers are finally at her doorstep. Allen Filters, Inc.—a producer of oil-cleanup products and services that Allen runs with her mother—may have little in terms of name recognition, but Allen says her journeys have convinced her that a small company can make it overseas. "If they have a good foundation," she says, "I think the world is open to most small businesses," she says. Foremost, the company must understand the markets and its customers.

Additionally, paperwork can take its toll on entrepreneurs trying to line up trade financing to pay for manufacturing abroad or to extend credit to customers.

This makes for the stiffest challenge of all and is exacerbated further by the reluctance of U.S. banks to jump into the fray. Remember that bankers' mistakes are often measured in millions of dollars, and after the impact of the Latin American loan debacle in the 1980s (to cite one example), some are still shaking. Besides that, even small foreign trade deals can often be complex. Jeanne A. Hulit, vice president for international banking at KeyBank of Maine, a unit of KeyCorp, says one recent small trade loan—less than $100,000—took so much of her time and energy that she might require an up-front fee from exporters in the future. This practice could easily become a trend, and is yet another factor that entrepreneurs should figure into the cost of running an export business.

An opportunity that companies with cash to spend have taken is vertical integration, or expanding the business by moving into other areas of the industry. Entrepreneurs can make investments into foreign distributorships, or the distributorships can be bought outright, enabling the exporter to gain closer proximity to his or her customers in that country. Benefits include better servicing of goods, which gives the buyer an edge over the competition while granting him or her extra international credibility. Eli E. Hertz, founder of Hertz Computer Corp. in New York, bought a small distributor in Israel in 1990 to sell his equipment. He says that being nearby to handle his clients' servicing needs gives him an edge over rival exporters. By positioning itself locally, Hertz is able to provide same-day service to some of its customers, an offering that sets their business apart from many other exporters. Today, Israeli customers account for 25 percent of Hertz's $10 million in sales.

However, for the typical small company, obtaining a foreign partner or entering into an agreement with a distributor is the preferred and less capital-intensive method to accessing a new market. And it's a crucial relationship.

Lazy distributors won't do much for business, while inept or unsavory ones will ruin a small company's reputation. Fortunately, finding a distributor does not necessarily mean a lot of legwork. Domestic companies selling related products can often provide a goldmine of information. Fred Hansen, vice-president for marketing at Mardel Laboratories, Inc. in Glendale Heights, Illinois (makers of water conditioners and other supplies for tropical-fish aquariums), hired a distributor in Hong Kong after contacting Penn Plax Plastics, Inc., a Garden City, New York firm that sells plastic underwater plants. The company didn't compete with Mardel, but it knew both the distributor and the industry well. Sharing this information was equally beneficial to both companies, yielding Penn Plax Plastics a deposit in its favor bank and Mardel an overseas distributor.

Selecting Foreign Allies

Distributors are the most common and widely used form of entry into international trade. Small to mid-sized businesses—short of starting a wholly-owned subsidiary—will find this the most reasonable path towards going global. Generally, only multinationals and a handful of larger companies (those with ample funds and/or a product lines that are instant winners) will be able to establish an independent footing in a foreign country from the outset. Mustering the financial wherewithal and the human resources needed to do so is just too difficult an endeavor for the small business. So until your business grows up into a multinational, the foreign distributor will remain the backbone of your export business.

Distribution is broadly defined as packaging, pricing, promoting and merchandising a product. It has been called the flipside of marketing. The fate of an overseas business is intimately related to the company's distribution methods—that is, to the company's distributor. A well chosen distributor will help you avoid faulty or faltering promotion from middlepersons. It will also help reduce the high freight costs of moving goods from the factory. And perhaps most important, it will better position a product or service to accommodate a foreign country's needs and culture. In other words, the distributor should help you take the first step toward good marketing, and at the same time establish a perception of the product that is as favorable as that which it has stateside.

Just as there are two basic approaches to foreign marketing (discussed later, in Chapter 6) distribution can also be classified as passive and active (or "direct").

Passive Distribution

Entrepreneurs who choose passive distribution allow someone to push their product or service for them. Of course, there is direct, day-to-day involvement, but for the most part, a representative creates the foreign inroads. Passive distribution is a very close cousin to passive marketing. Both benefit from very low up-front costs. And the drawbacks are the same—and plentiful. Without control of its goods, a business is in the dark. Managers are unable to adequately forecast demand or the lack thereof. Opportunity costs are high, as a lazy or incompetent rep, or one that has a "hotter" and similar product to sell, may not be finding all the markets that exists for your product. Should the export begin to take off—stirring management enough to go direct—the exporter may find that it must rebuild its entire strategy. A rep's job is to build a name for your business by finding a market for the product, and should you pull your product from your rep's lines, he or she is going to find and tout a replacement. In essence, you could very well be be creating competition for your very own goods.

Reasons for avoiding passive distribution go on and on. Suffice it to say most are tied directly to an exporter being somewhat powerless in the sought after marketplace. However, for the tightly budgeted business that is eager to enter the foreign marketplace, passive distribution may be the only option. See Chapter 6 for more information on the pitfalls of passive distribution. Of course, the well-capitalized business usually has more options when choosing a method of distribution, and the direct route is strongly encouraged.

Direct Distribution

Direct distribution is fast, efficient, and also more expensive than passive distribution. The active methods described below involve meeting prospective foreign distributors abroad. By directly involving the business owner in the selection process, such means often prove to be vastly more fruitful. The ultimate selection of distributors takes place as the result of face-to-face meetings between the exporter and distribution managers.

Usually nothing can adequately replace this kind of direct experience since the interviewer can apply both intuitive and intellectual skills. It's the confluence of these that so often leads to a satisfactory result—whether the meetings are brokered by the DOC or arranged entirely by the business itself. Following are descriptions of a few ways for entrepreneurs to actively meet foreign distributors.

Matchmakers. A trade delegation of top U.S. executives heads to (for example) Europe to visit a few selected countries. In each country visited, local DOC officers eagerly roll out the red carpet. They will largely arrange meetings, factory visits, symposia, and even dinner banquets. Figure on a cost of roughly $4,000 to $6,000. The relatively high expense means that this method is often most attractive to established

Matchmakers are often used in high-end industries such as aerospace.

companies in highly visible industries like aerospace, computers, biomedical equipment, etc. Conversely, matchmakers are usually not the optimal route for a small company whose first priority is to nominally enter a foreign market.

Trade Shows/Missions. The DOC regularly conducts shows that promote a specific industry overseas. Such events allow local managers and businessmen to examine products they may be interested in buying or representing. Additionally, opportunities abound for interfacing on the exhibition floor, where business relationships can be established and may flourish. Many exporters have found that the deals made at missions such as these could, over time, lead to profitable ventures. However, like the matchmaker program, this is an expensive way for a small company with limited resources to scout a distributor (though exhibition space can be shared).

The DOC also runs a trade show promoting "made in the U.S.A." (MITU) products and services. These shows usually travel to a new country each month and cover more than one industry. In the Middle East, for example, MITU trade shows are usually conducted according to the following schedule: Dubai, May; Kuwait, June; Saudi Arabia, September; Dubai, October; and Bahrain, Qatar, and Oman, November. Participation runs about $8,000 per show. This does not include expenses for travel and lodging.

Agent Distributor Service. The ADS constitutes the biggest "bang for the buck," and is perhaps the best service the DOC offers the small company poised to go global. Excluding the OBR and the CSS (see the Appendix), no other service offers as good a return on investment. Typically, the procedure begins when the business owner has narrowed down the choices of the country or countries he or she wishes to enter. The DOC presently runs the ADS service in 107 countries, so most countries of potential interest are likely to be covered. Thereafter, the business forwards its product catalogs and price lists on to their assigned ADS agent. From there, the agent will scout, search, and locate local distributors who may express interest in representing the product line. Having viewed the business's catalogs, a local distributor will advise the U.S. attaché accordingly. This process will be repeated a few times by the attaché, terminating once a list has been compiled of the local foreign distributors most eager to meet with the business.

Before you can participate in the ADS program, you'll need to call the DOC district office nearest you (there are 72 in the U.S.) and request form ITA 424P. Besides the customary request for a profile of your company, the form asks that you list: (1) The kinds of contacts you seek in the market or country of your choice (i.e., agent or distributor) and be exacting in detailing the type of distribution you want and don't want; (2) The product or service you wish to export; and (3) The main qualifications (sales, technical, etc.) desired of the candidate for the job. You must submit the ADS form in duplicate, and prepare only one ADS package for each market. Each ADS package must be accompanied by a minimum of five catalogs or brochures for small markets like New Zealand, and 11 to 20 catalogs for larger markets like Japan, France, or Germany. The brochures must reveal the products your business wants to market in that country, and be accompanied by a price list, in order to give the foreign distributor an idea of the saleability of and market for your products.

Write an introductory letter, remembering that the foreign distributor reading it will want to know as much about your company as possible. Above all, be practical and get to the essentials. Give the what, how, where, when, who, and why of your products. The distributor is weighing the business advantages of taking on your product, so it's vital to convey the appropriate attitude in your written presentation. Your initial goal is to open doors, so be clear and concise

about your product's merits. Sales will take care of themselves later on.

There is also a "gold key" ADS that is faster than the standard service. It offers secretarial and interpreter services as needed, and comes at a slightly higher fee. Exporters often take advantage of the service, as under normal circumstances, up to three months may pass before you receive a list of the distributors you are seeking.

Once you do receive the list, however, it should conclude your initial step, and the rest will be up to you. Do not assume, however, that the foreign companies from the list are uniformly well-suited for the task. Recall from the information requested on form ITA 424P that you should indicate the kind of network of distributors you need to do justice to your product(s). Also, give the DOC an idea of how to narrow down your choices by forwarding a list of the distributors with whom you do not wish to establish contact. It's important to clearly define the channel of distribution you must have, otherwise you may have waited three months for nothing. Still, the ADS works well and at a low cost when one considers the saving in direct expenses related to the fees incurred for food, lodging, transportation, and finding a foreign distributor.

Selecting a Distributor

Suppose that you've forwarded form ITA-424P to the DOC. A few months have passed and you've received a list of candidates vying for the distribution of your product in your selected markets. You should now begin to plan your first trip overseas for the purpose of visiting and evaluating those candidates.

Normally, a business allocates at least two days for each country to be visited, with a half day allotted for each distributor to be interviewed. For those markets that are extremely important, like the U.K., France, Germany, and Brazil, plan two extra days. For a market that is in a league by itself (e.g., Japan) schedule one to two weeks.

Before you arrive, send a letter officially introducing yourself and your company, and outlining your business plan. Suggest a day and hour for the proposed meeting, plotting out the specific activities within the schedule. Include your company's profile (age, size, ownership) and further explain your product or products: Their functions and limitations; their customary channel of distribution; the overall benefit your company can offer to the market; and what your competitors (both domestic and international) offer. Also describe any special handling your products may require, and how your products can make the local distributor a leader in the industry. Finally, include a brief explanation of the overall philosophy of your company and its marketing goals and objectives. Make sure that each distributor gets a personalized copy of the letter.

The foreign distributor will, in the crucial first years, either cultivate fertile soil for the product lines or imperceptibly build up a negative image. Once you set foot in the country where you wish to do business, the window of opportunity is small and crucial—when you visit, you will have only a few hours to glean the true motivations of each potential distributor and to evaluate its capacity, creditworthiness, and credibility. Prior to your departure from the U.S., you would be well advised to draw up a distributor profile listing the priorities that ought to be reviewed and evaluated with each of the candidates visited. Rate them accordingly during or after the trip. By the same token, you should confer with others in your company, both your superiors and staff, to evaluate the strength(s) and weaknesses of your company and define the risks inherent in the decisions you will shortly have to make. Specifically, what are

your company's foremost priorities in undertaking this new business endeavor?

Build a framework around what you want out of the distributor. Recognize just what it is they do. Logistically, they bring your products to the shores of their country, making sure everything clears Customs and is warehoused. Commercially, a distributor will price, promote, sell and, if needed, service these products. Financially, it will collect the monies derived from these sales and will remit them (in U.S. dollars) to your company. And conceptually, it will create, develop, and establish a perception of the product and your company among local customers.

The logistic, commercial, and financial missions described above are the easiest for the distributor to comprehend because they are tangible. The fourth—creating a perception—is much harder to grasp because it is intangible. Yet, when all is said and done, it is the distributor's mastery of the fourth mission that will determine your long-term success.

The Distributor Interview: A Checklist

Once you and the officers of your company have defined your business's long-term international marketing plan, the time has come to review the kinds of criteria on which you will base selection of the best distributor for the job. The following are twelve important considerations:

The distributor's perception of the market. Each distributor has a different perception of their local market. By lumping and averaging all their market evaluations, you should get a fair overall view. Correlate this data with what you received from the DOC (trade statistics, industry analysis, country marketing plans) and with the information in your privately prepared market survey (see Chapter 6). The truth on market conditions should begin to seep out of the averages—leading you to pick the distributor whose market perception is closest to what you perceive as accurate. However, you must also take into account the "human element" within distributor perceptions. The distributor providing an overly favorable market evaluation may be a fool, or may be a real go-getter. The one implying an unduly pessimistic evaluation may be a realist or may, in truth, lack dynamism and aggressiveness. It comes down to face-to-face contact and intuition. There is no substitute for either.

General information about the distributor. How big and how old is the company visited? What are your overall impressions of the premises? Are they clean, functional, and modern, or messy, unwieldy, and outdated? Does the company give an impression of being fairly active and successful? Admittedly, appearances can be deceiving. But your ears should prick up if a distributor is telling you it's going to set the market on fire with your product—yet everything you see provides evidence to the contrary. Take the example of one exporter's experience with the manager of a distribution company in Cairo. The manager did his best during the interview to convince the exporter that his company was the best suited for the job. Meanwhile, during the meeting, the exporter could see salesmen sleeping at their desks.

Of course, different lands live under different rules, and cultural differences can, to a certain extent, influence office conduct. In Europe, there is in general, a clear delineation of titles and power. In Asia, you may find the president of the company in shirtsleeves working in the corner of a busy office cluttered with various desks. Latin American offices are generally less formally structured than offices in the U.S., and while the atmosphere may at times convey an overall impression of amateurism, in truth the cultural differences in no way undermine their level of professionalism. This is also true of some countries in the Middle East. Take time to separate the serious candidates from the flimsy ones. This skill comes with experience. And if, given your experience, you're moving at a faster pace than you're comfortable with, step back and get advice.

The distributor's knowledge of your industry and local and international regulations governing it. It might seem obvious, but the successful candidate must know your industry and the local and international laws governing it. Common sense or not, international trade is replete with sagas of products that bombed miserably in a market because they were handled by unsuitable distributors.

Product lines already represented. Do not be so short-sighted or unprofessional as to give your product lines to a foreign distributor handling a competitive line, regardless

Finding a good foreign distributor can make your venture more likely to succeed.

Distributor Checklist

- ☐ Does the distributor have a good sense of the marketplace?
- ☐ Does the company seem successful? Is it small or large?
- ☐ What is the distributor's knowlege of the industry and its regulations?
- ☐ What other product lines is he/she representing?
- ☐ What type of resources is the distributor willing to offer?
- ☐ What will the advertising and promotions department do?
- ☐ What are the warehousing capabilities?

of the distributor's glowing promises. Justice will not be done to your line. Also be wary of the distributor vying for your product line as another extension of a "package." Your products could be buried in that package and take a backseat to others, thereby devaluing your investment of time and money. Finally, insist that your product or service be handled by someone within the firm who has the relevant experience.

Desire for exclusivity of distribution. Be apprehensive of a distributor who does not ask for an exclusive. A distributor worth its salt will always ask for an exclusive, because properly establishing a product will demand time, labor, and money. The distributor will have to print brochures outlining the features and benefits of your products, warehouse the products, allocate working capital, and educate his or her salespeople as well as the market. The rewards, if they do come, will not be immediate.

American companies are known overseas for playing "mean and lean"—that is, giving the distribution of their products to more than one distributor, sometimes unbeknownst to all players. This is ultimately shortsighted. Most products have everything to gain by exclusive distribution. In addition, a policy of nonexclusivity of distribution in a few foreign markets will demand additional staff work at home and duplication of effort, hence higher costs.

Sales organization, number of salespeople, geographic coverage, pricing. Simply put, in international trade you are going to kiss a lot of frogs before you meet the princely distributor of your dreams. You are entering the international arena as a relatively small business. Some of the foreign distributors you will meet will also be small, others will be well-established and successful. Careful, though—that may only be because their product lines are well established and they may not really need your business.

The vast majority of distributors, however, are a good deal newer to the game, can be one-person shows, and will be eager to take on your products. Usually they consist of a former salesman or a sales manager striking out on his or her own as the quintessential entrepreneur.

Since you will not have the time to be in the field with the distributor's salespeople (the best way to judge its sales force) you will have to ask, probe, and question: How many salespeople will promote the product line? When do the salespeople call and what's the frequency of their calls? To whom do they sell? Will they call regularly on your main potential customers, or will your product line be part of an overall package? How is the sales force divided—into account lines, customer lines, geographic lines? How will they price your product? This point in particular must be discussed thoroughly. If you set too high a price, your distributor will skim a market, resulting in trifling sales. (Different rules apply to luxury goods, where a high price may to some extent define the value perceived by the market).

Promotions and advertising. Does the distributor candidate conduct promotion programs on behalf of products like yours? Of what nature? How often? Will your products also be promoted? How is this promotion conducted? What about cooperative advertising? Will the distributor translate English copy into the local language? Is it willing to share or cover the cost of this step? Will the overall message of your advertising be respected and conveyed? Will the distributor sell direct, or through subdistribution? In general, continent-sized countries (e.g., Australia, Indonesia, India, Zaire, Nigeria, Mexico, Brazil) require some kind of subdistribution. Heavily populated but geographically smaller countries like the Netherlands, Japan, and Taiwan require a direct distribution system. And there are third- and fourth-tier levels of distribution as well. For instance, Italy, with its Mezzo Giorno, or Germany, with its 17 lenders, have several different markets that demand subdistributors along with smaller distributors who work with them.

Physical capacity/warehousing. What qualifies a good distributor, among other things, is its capacity and willingness to warehouse products. In many countries, when you ask a distributor to show you its "warehouse," do not be surprised to see (especially in Latin America, Africa and poorer Asian countries) a hole-in-the-wall where boxes are fighting for meager space. If you ask, "Is that all?," undoubtedly you will hear that the distributor has another location. However, if your company carries a line of specialty goods that demand second-to-none warehousing or, say, refrigeration, you must confirm the distributor's claims. Products like pharmaceuticals or perishable foods won't stand a chance under poor warehousing conditions.

Ability to provide aftermarket service. Mechanical or electrical equipment, along with other select products, need aftermarket service. Therefore, a good distributor, eager to represent a technical line, should have a technical department for this purpose. Never make the error of awarding distribution rights to your products based on a distributor's assurance that "We will soon get a service engineer just for your products!"

Any marketing manager worth his or her salt knows that establishing a brand name is a demanding and painstaking task, and also knows that poor service will blow it. Basically, three subcriteria qualify a foreign distributor to provide adequate aftermarket service (that is, if these criteria are met, you are probably dealing with a servicing professional): (a) An adequate service staff that is able to interpret and understand English diagrams/service manuals and to perform the necessary repairs; (b) A willingness of the distributor to stock, at its expense, necessary spare parts; (c) A willingness of the distributor to send an engineer stateside to attend in-depth training classes, following the rigorous guidelines used in the domestic market.

Success in developing brand loyalty. Brand loyalty is the surest and fastest way to achieve long-term success. A recent study by the Boston Consulting Group found that out of 30 brands that were number one in their product category in 1930, 27 of them were still topping the charts in the 1990s. A new brand faces many obstacles at the outset of its introduction—it can easily become snubbed, ignored, and may ultimately die. For this reason, entering a market the right way at the right time is one of the most important aspects of a successful international marketing strategy. Initially selecting the best distributor for the job is the first and most important step of any strategy.

Reputation with suppliers, customers, and banks (credit rating). This is a difficult attribute to assess, but its importance is abundantly clear. The best method to determine a reputation is to talk to people, even if it means adding days to your travel schedule. If at all possible, ask to speak with existing customers. Surely, you'll be directed to the happiest of the lot, but take the opportunity to ask these customers some straightforward questions, such as: Are you satisfied with your distributor? If yes, why? If no, why? Does it deliver on time? Does it service the goods properly? Duly note the responses to these questions and use them later on in reaching your decision.

In international trade, as in other professions, a kind of fraternity of export managers exists whom you can query and who may gladly help you out. As for creditworthiness, references generally provided by banks are so bland and vague as to be useless.

Recruit an able and skilled service staff.

To have the clearest picture, you must look elsewhere. This process will usually bring you back to seeking references from the U.S. companies in your industry that are supplying your candidate(s).

General attributes. Evaluate your distributor's trustworthiness, readiness to order, ability to forecast sales, and marketing techniques/objectives. First things first: Make sure that your distributor acknowledges that it can be trusted never to repackage your products under its name for export to other foreign markets. Deceptions such as this have been known to happen with unscrupulous distributors. Also, avoid making requests for stocking orders. This may be perceived as unfair on your part by the distributor, who will want to see what the market will bear. Otherwise, always keep in mind the possibility that your distributor will not meet sales objectives. Of course, you can fire an unsuccessful distributor, but this is an expensive proposition as

you will have to select from among the initial candidates all over again.

Persist and Use Your Business Sense. Going global is not for everyone. It's hard work and will take a tremendous amount of effort on your part. Sorting through and making sense out of the paperwork and bureaucracy associated with foreign business can be a daunting process, let alone the risk associated with entering any new marketplace. If you don't do the initial homework, the information essential to your decision may seem either painfully inadequate, or incomprehensible and overwhelming in size and volume. What is available will no doubt come from the DOC. Although this agency is there to assist you, it's still part of a bureaucracy where pinpointing information is often difficult.

As you've seen in this chapter, while several factors have eased previously restrictive and expensive barriers to stepping abroad, don't think that means there is a golden path laid out for you to float along on your way to spoon-fed profits. Scams, in the form of export diversions and others, abound. Knowledge of your targeted market is a must. And completing your due diligence is absolutely necessary. A deeper glance into the above criteria should tell you that this is nothing new. You've encountered it all right here at home. Entry into, and success within, overseas markets is a matter of hard work and persistence, just like it is domestically. And like anyone in business anywhere, be prepared for a truly expensive lesson or two. John P. Wooley, general manager of PC Industries, recalls how he shipped a $10,000 replacement computer component to a French customer. He was stunned when he was billed $2,500 for value-added tax. Wooley's company had to absorb the unexpected bill, forcing him to rethink the company's overseas commitment. The incident could likely have been avoided by a thorough examination of French tax laws, done internally or through consultation with a knowledgeable tax professional.

An abundance of free market information, useful in identifying suitable markets, can usually be had for the asking. Many firms use the DOC or unrelated federal agencies for this information. Furthermore, a crucial second tier of resources exists in state-sponsored export promotion programs. Finally, an abundance of free or cheap information for going global is available on the Internet. For listings, please refer to the Appendix at the back of this book.

Chapter 2

The Downsizing Phenomenon

Depending on who you talk to, downsizing is either a great boon for business or a heartless corporate move. While downsizing—and the corporate chiefs who set it in motion—get their share of bad press during recessionary times, the process also achieves worthy and necessary outcomes. Reduced labor costs, increased profit margins, and restored life for ailing or uncompetitive companies allows businesses the possibility of rehiring in future years. An advocate of downsizing might very well point stateside for evidence supporting his or her stance. Hirings are up, unemployment has dwindled, and real wages have recently seen an increase—the business environment is more robust than ever.

An appraisal of the global economy will also bear out such positive examples as Southeast Asia. Once recognized as the home of armies of cheap, unskilled labor, where discardable toys and throw-away transistor radios were manufactured, Southeast Asia is poised to become the next business center of the world—according to trend-watcher and author John Naisbitt, who believes

Workers in the future will bring more skills and a greater adaptability to their companies.

the region will also have an economic, political, and cultural influence. Beyond U.S. shores, downsizing, restructuring, and the Westernization of economies will continually mold a powerful new global workforce with increasingly sophisticated skills. Multinational companies and start-up entrepreneurs alike are beginning to see the opportunities in taking their products and businesses to these regions. Labor has survived and even flourished with technical training provided by business and government. Consider, too, the increasing numbers of multilingual business school graduates who possess a combination of business savvy and multicultural depth and are now positioned to enter foreign markets and tap this wealth of labor.

Research shows that the workers who remain after downsizing and restructuring, and those who become newly available to businesses, will expand their skills and grow with the needs of the company. Not unlike Charles Darwin's model—originally intended to encompass only the plant and animal kingdom—downsizing and restructurings

see to it that only the fittest survive. Social scientists may balk, but it is a law of nature. Nevertheless, responsible governments in most of the emerging markets are seeing to it that those left behind are retrained for adaptation to a changing workplace. Though the financial benefits of downsizing can be overestimated (and likewise, the burden on remaining employees underestimated), there is one inarguable outcome: Downsizing has a healthy effect on the skills and initiative of the labor market.

The new breed of worker is fast shrinking the gap between experience levels and wages throughout the developing and less-developed world. Skilled workers compete on a far more equal footing than before. Far Eastern workers in particular are now poised not only to participate in manufacturing, but are providing input into creative product development and business services as well. Others that have been displaced from industry, the military, and even government positions are learning new skills and participating more productively later in their careers.

A case in point is Israel's high-tech boom, now pushing the country's economic growth to around six percent a year.

Israel's homegrown military technology is now seeping into the civilian market—due to a downturn in defense spending coming on the heels of cooling tensions with Arab neighbors. Workers are leaving defense manufacturers and elite units of the Israel Defense Force (IDF) to form companies of their own. And they are bringing with them top technology and entrepreneurial zeal. Says Benny Landa of Indigo, a leader in digital printing technology, "We have become an atomic reactor of ideas, technology, and entrepreneurship." The ideas and technology that Landa touts have thrived in Israel for years, but what's new is the entrepreneurship. The reason: Downsizing, in such areas as Israel's vaunted defense contracting companies and elsewhere, forced a "retooling" of the labor force. The result was a boost to the Israeli economy that helped cut the jobless rate to under 7 percent in 1995 from 11 percent two years before.

Further affecting the trend is the relatively recent arrival of 600,000 immigrants from the former Soviet Union, many of them highly trained in technical fields. Whereas a mass of immigration this size would normally send jitters through a country of only five million people, the arrival of the ex-Soviets has proved to be a blessing to labor.

How Downsizing Affects the Marketplace

Displaced workers will often strike out on their own in a downsized/restructured industry or company, as seen in the Israeli industrial-military shakedown over recent years. Whether acting as hired-gun executives, consultants, or freelancers, these enterprising workers also eagerly train, adopt, and apply new techniques to their trades and services. This evolution mutually benefits the healthy and sick economies of the world. For example, the U.S. economy enjoyed a rock-bottom "natural" unemployment rate of only 5.3 percent, with a record 0.8 percent rise in average hourly wages during June 1996. But if U.S. companies are now facing an undeniable upswing in demand for products and services, at least they can court new employees without sacrificing their downsizing gains—a trend likely to become commonplace.

Japan presents a compelling example of the changes destined to make over national work forces due to the labor shakeout. Employment security is slowly fading with Japan's recent recession, the rise of the yen against the dollar, and the end of the Cold War. For the most part, Japanese policies and regulations prohibit the kind of wholesale layoffs common in the U.S., but that hasn't stopped corporate Japan from finding ways to circumvent costly policies. Companies like Sony, Fujitsu, Toshiba, and Matsushita Electric, once longtime customers of smaller Japanese suppliers, have begun to abandon them for less expensive Southeast Asian suppliers, a move that market-seeking U.S. entrepreneurs and exporters are acting on. These once nationalistic Japanese concerns are moving factories offshore, relentlessly squeezing subcontractors for ever lower costs, and spurning traditional ways of doing business in favor of bigger profit margins. Companies of all sizes have little choice but to introduce exacting new job performance standards and merit pay in order to stay competitive within the restructuring of the once benign business standard. Further, because regulations in Japan make it hard to fire workers or provide less than generous severance packages, middle-aged, highly paid Japanese managers are being harassed and bullied to quit. Only recently, men aged 45 to 54—the least technically skilled group in the Japanese economy—were

Younger workers, as seen throughout Asia, are uniquely equipped to take on the challenges of the information age workplace.

actually the most highly paid. Now, they constitute Japan's fastest-growing group of unemployed, their ranks swelling to 37.5 percent in 1995. So continues the brutal shakeout, though as noted above, in an economy forced to restructure, "older" workers forced to retrain are benefited by their newly acquired vocational skills in the long run.

Contrast the case of middle-aged managers in Japan to that of young workers throughout Asia—superbly qualified to undertake the new jobs produced by the information economy. These employees are also working at a fraction of the cost of traditional programmers and designers stateside. Nearly anywhere in Asia nowadays, locals perform the same highly skilled tasks one would expect to find in Palo Alto, Boston, or Tokyo. Frugally minded U.S. managers have noticed. As discussed later in Chapter 6, American companies are taking their manufacturing overseas by way of joint ventures, branch offices, subsidiaries, and through contract manufacturing—wherein the hands-on work is farmed out to a foreign company.

Perhaps the best known joint venture of an American high-tech company and an Asian facility with superlative talent is the Silicon Graphics Inc. operation in Bangalore, India. Software designers there earn $300 a month—middle-class wages in India, though well below the poverty level in the U.S. They develop, among others, programs that produce three-dimensional images for diagnosing brain disorders. In Singapore, where wages are similar to those in India, native engineers design future generations of personal digital assistants for Hewlett-Packard Co. In Taiwan, Hong Kong, and South China, research and development teams are at work on multimedia gizmos ranging from digital answering machines to interactive computers for children. At Bilingual Education Computing, Inc., in Beijing, China, artists, engineers, and programmers are building interactive CD-ROMs, complete with voice and animation, for the teaching of English. So far they have sold over 50,000 copies at $55 apiece. However, writing the scripts, the most creative part of the process, is done in Taiwan (where labor is higher priced). But the mainland continues to happily grab the more tedious, routine work on the product—from animation to voice-over recording.

In general, workers in emerging nations are doing sophisticated high-tech jobs for a lot less pay than their First World counterparts receive. According to the Union Bank of Switzerland, not only do the wage and yearly earnings gaps between East and West remain vast, but the Eastern workers log more hours yearly. In the East, business professions such as engineering, management, and banking are much more modestly paid. This phenomenon has consequently created a plentiful supply of workers who choose and train for high-tech jobs. It doesn't matter that most are coming in from overseas multinationals and smaller companies just now gaining a foothold in their country. The stream of labor into the high-tech marketplace will also help to hold down wages, at least for the near-term. Ultimately, most experts agree, there will be a shift toward a worldwide equivalency of wages.

The Trend: Offshore Labor

The inexorable political shift to market economies, the spread of higher education, and decades of overseas training by multinationals mean that now, an increasingly better balance of skills exists worldwide. Suddenly, legions of overseas workers are capable of performing tasks once solely associated with white-collar Western workers. And because of advances in telecommunications, these workers have become more accessible than ever before.

In the 1970s and '80s, the West discovered the benefits in shifting production offshore. In the '90s, we're learning about shifting knowledge-based labor offshore. Even cities far away from the innovators and end-users, like Taipei, Edinburgh, Singapore, and Penang, Malaysia, are emerging as global product development centers. Witnessing the success of such areas, other centers are sprouting throughout Asia and the world, whereby vast pools of labor are made available to Westerners by means of open-door policies.

Many of the lessons companies are learning about the high-tech sector of the global workforce are applicable to the service sector as well. This sector is the West's other truly big job generator: The Japanese may have their electronics and the Germans their manufacturing, but when it comes to command of global markets, the U.S. owns and dominates service. North America is the world leader in exporting everything from data security to crowd control. The 1995 surplus in services amounted to about $60 billion, even accounting for a recent slight downturn.

To manage data and develop products for its global financial services, Citibank relies on local skills in India, Hong Kong, Australia, and Singapore. Houston-based M.W. Kellogg farms out detailed architectural-engineering work for power and chemical plants to a Mexican partner. Anupam P. Puri, managing director of McKinsey & Co.'s Bombay office, says that such task transfers are long overdue. "Most of our multinational clients are still very far behind in seeing how they can redistribute service work around the world," he says.

The true potential of offshore skilled labor is just beginning to be tapped. For years, companies such as American Airlines and Citicorp have loaded tons of documents onto planes bound for low-paid keypunch operators in the Dominican Republic or the Philippines. U.S. law firms, ad agencies, and nonprofit groups cut documentation costs by hiring outsourcers such as International Data Solutions, Inc. (IDS), in Herndon, Virginia, an employer of thousands of workers in the Philippines. And now, it's becoming increasingly common to contract-out overseas workers for higher-end services. In this respect, the business world is clearly moving toward a placeless society.

Although regulatory hurdles remain, the technological barriers to the placeless society are falling fast. IDS, for example, scans case and client files for U.S. law firms and beams them digitally via satellite to the Philippines. There, workers organize and index the files. A U.S. worker then retrieves them via a computer network. For this task, IDS employs two full-time U.S.-based workers and upwards of 3,000 Filipinos. "This trend is accelerating dramatically," says IDS president Kenneth R. Short. "It really doesn't matter where the work is done as long as quality, price, and service are right."

On the other hand, for higher-tech, more highly skilled labor, the savings

in using Third World labor can easily be overestimated—because in the creative parts of a design or production process, stateside engineers may still be preferred, even though their labor may cost a premium. Of course, such expenditures are part of any company's business plan, wherein ratios are devised to determine where the bulk of expenditures are being made—in design or in production. If the main costs are incurred in production, big savings could occur by going global on the back-end of product development—the often tedious work of turning a conceptual design into blueprints, computer codes, working models, and in testing the final product.

Recall the example of the Taiwanese designers at Bilingual shipping off their "busy work" to the mainland. Subbing out the more tedious work there allows them to realize huge savings. The mainland Chinese accept lower wages, ranging from $75 a month

Multinational companies are exploring new ways to redistribute work to emerging markets.

for a keypunch operator to $400 for a good artist. Typically, this subbed-out work amounts to about 80 percent of the labor involved in producing software for CD-ROM products. Production costs are anywhere from a quarter to a tenth of what the same work in the U.S. would require, so the savings are high. A further advantage is that although the particular software designed features the English language, none of the back-end staff need to know or understand English in order to complete their portion of the work. This benefit is borne out in the case of Bilingual's product.

On the flipside, these "advances" in global production leave millions of American workers—software designers, bookkeepers, mechanical engineers, draftsmen, librarians, and more— in a vulnerable position. In a sense, however, the flow of jobs out of one region into another will be a temporary phenomenon. As global business expansion continues, job candidates everywhere will soon be sought by employers everywhere. The wage gap is bound to close eventually, as technicians and engineers in the developing world command higher wages and regional pay discrepancies level out. It's instructive to look to Israel, where one of the country's early advantages, the lower cost of labor, is diminishing. In the 1980s, the pay gap between Israel and Silicon Valley was so great— around 40 percent for top programmers—that big U.S. investors like Intel, IBM, and Motorola were running into the marketplace. But with the increase in demand, wages rose and the differential narrowed. Graduates of Haifa's Technion are now stepping out of school into $45,000 yearly salaries, not much less than their U.S. counterparts. Some experienced Israeli programmers are even commanding Silicon Valley rates. Still, on average a 20 percent difference in wages does exist and will continue for some time to be enough of an incentive to draw foreign investors and import-exporters.

Companies that are tactically and financially equipped to move operations are finding cheaper labor in Asia. As of 1994, the Pacific Tiger countries averaged about $5.81 per hour for manufacturing jobs, compared to Germany's 1994 rate of $27.37 or the U.S.'s $17.10. Mexico anchors the competitive wages scale with an average of $2.57 per hour, a number dragged even lower by the devalued peso. The hourly wage of Japanese workers—$21.83—stands as an example of the impact of the increasing power of Japanese business and currency. It wasn't too long ago that the Japanese market was sought out for its cheap labor pools, a trend that has solidly reversed itself as the Japanese economy has undergone massive restructuring and explosive growth.

Remember, the information superhighway is a two-way street that not only allows U.S. and European engineers to compete for work in Asia, but also the reverse. Again, Japan presents an example of the crucial changes coming to pass. Because of the terrific rise of the yen through late 1995, which would otherwise have gutted Japanese competitiveness abroad, firms have scrambled to build cars in their overseas markets, buying more parts abroad and hiring foreign workers to assemble the vehicles. The end of the Cold War and the collapse of the socialist system also helped Japan's higher priced workers maintain their salaries despite the international trend toward cheaper labor. Meanwhile, far-reaching trade agreements are opening up the nation's most protected and least efficient industries, such as agriculture. But Japan will clearly not abandon its post-World War II economic miracle. It is again entering a period of restructuring, retooling, and retraining, just in time to join and remain competitive in the new, widely skilled global workforce.

In the future, graduates of American business schools will be one kind of job candidate that the Far East will find most difficult to duplicate—largely as they rethink earlier theories that strategic thinking should take a second place to inexpensive labor. Because marketing and creativity will always be in high demand, brighter graduates will be sought out and will continue to receive stagger ing first-year salaries. Candidates with bilingual or even trilingual abilities will find themselves in even hotter demand as the global marketplace becomes increasingly competitive.

Chapter 3

The Ripple Effect of Privatization

As financially squeezed foreign governments seek to raise money through the privatization of government-run businesses, opportunities for the institutional investor will begin to trickle down to the competitive entrepreneur entering the marketplace. Germany, France, China, and Mexico plan to offer American investors the chance to take part in huge privatizations over the next few years. And beyond these major areas for commerce, lesser known entities such as Argentina, Brazil, India, Indonesia, Poland, South Africa, South Korea, and Turkey are shaping up to be key players in the future of international trade. As a result, the surge in the capitalization of overseas funds show little sign of abating. InterSec Research Corp., a financial consultant group in Stamford, Connecticut, estimates that United States' pension funds' international assets will reach $725 billion by 2000, double what they are today. Even within the current climate of uncertainty, U.S. institutional investors remain convinced that roaming the globe in search of portfolio diversification is ultimately safer than putting all their eggs in the blue chip baskets at home.

A number of changes will take place as privatization in foreign markets becomes more widespread. Cozy backroom deals made between cronies will diminish, as a greater sense of duty among managers seeking to keep their jobs promotes a more aggressive pursuit of the market share. Shareholder activists will push companies to boost profits and dividends, oust poor management, and scrap executive pay plans not tied to performance. Shareholder defense committees will fight for their rights in court, and even seek basic securities law changes. Even Europe's holding companies, famous for entrenched management, will urge companies to boost returns.

How well chummy European management stalwarts will answer this wake-up call remains hard to say. But with the recent victories of shareholder activists, they will find it difficult to ignore the flood of changes.

Like any sweeping economic reform, the privatization movement has its winners and losers. Casualties in the war waged against sloth in the European community include the booting out of Compagnie de Suez Chairman Gerard Worms and the recent firing of Mac Fournier, Navigation Mixte founder and chairman for the past 26 years. Those who should consider these moves fair warning, say shareholder activists, include the heads of Deutsche Bank, Mediobanco, Banque Nationale de Paris, and British Telecommunications. And because most of the money flowing into foreign stock markets and privatizations is U.S. capital, these once stodgy companies must pay increasing attention to placating American investors. A new level of discipline is forcing managers to comply with more uniform standards of corporate accounting and disclosures, a trend that is beneficial to the company wishing to know more about its financial "dance partner."

Opportunities in the Global Marketplace

As the established trend of privatization spreads, particularly in Europe, Asia, and Latin America, a domino effect is being felt throughout the world. Look at what's happening in the telephone company industry worldwide. In 1993, Latvia, South Korea, and Singapore privatized their telecom markets. In 1994, Russia, Pakistan, Peru, and Hungary followed. Then in 1995 and 1996, the dominos really fell when twenty countries, including Bolivia, India, the Czech Republic, Indonesia, Thailand, Turkey, Uganda, Cape Verde, Cote d'Ivoire, Sri Lanka, Albania, Ghana, Guinea, Moldova, New Guinea, Nicaragua, Panama, Paraguay, Taiwan, and Zambia opened their markets. In 1997, El Salvador, Honduras, and Poland also intend to see their phone markets go private. Inevitably, countries elsewhere, even with centralized or socialist economies (such as China), will feel more pressure to open up their markets once the word is in on the success of the above countries. China, the world's most populous nation, wants to install 100 million digital lines by the end of the decade, at a cost of $40 billion. According to James R. Long, president of world trade for Canada's Northern Telecom, "China is the hottest opportunity in the world. Everybody is trying to get in there." China's goal is to expand the network of telecom lines from three lines per 100 people to eight in the next five years. That means installing a network the size of Bell Canada each and every year.

In nation after nation, a modern communications infrastructure is priming the economy for businesspeople worldwide to move in. Remember the maxim presented in Chapter 1—governments are overlooking political and ideological differences in favor of economic

China is considered one of the world's hottest markets.

unity. And with unity, and the lack of barriers, will come opportunity for both multinationals and entrepreneurs. As government slowly exits business, traditional channels of finding public sector work will be less useful to global companies. Freer markets level the playing field, forcing foreign companies to compete more aggressively and to seek less help from financing bodies and the governments themselves. However, privatizations will always be a good deal less swift and sure than private sell-offs. In this sense, foreign companies banking on privatizations for contracts may be disappointed. This is as true in the developed countries of Western Europe as it is in emerging, socialist or totalitarian economies. Politics, weak stock markets, union protests, and investor wariness easily create delays. But despite these unsteady variables, privatization payoffs remain quite alluring.

Benefits and Liabilities of Privatization

First, privatization brings in cash. European national governments have discovered that asset sales offer the best hope for slashing budget deficits. And cutting deficits is required for each country's full and fruitful participation in the EU. The deficits of EU countries currently average 4.5 percent of gross domestic product. However, in order for a country to be a party to its Monetary Union (EMU), the country's defecit cannot exceed the rigid standard of 3 percent of its GDP by the year 2000. Thus, the precautions described above that cause privatizations to unfold slowly could go by the wayside as countries hurry to meet the EMU's standards.

Second, privatization has a galvanizing effect on business in general. A country's industrial clout often hinges on privatization, which brings in new sources of cash, new productivity, and fresh faces. Companies become more competitive when they're independent. Indeed, sometimes a company's survival depends on its autonomy. Says an official of the French aluminum giant Pechiney, "We need capital to grow, and the state can't provide it." Perhaps that is why Pechiney is on the block.

On the other hand, sometimes a company takes the new infusion of capital and resolutely fails to work on its weaknesses. Take Telefonos de Mexico

(Telmex), Mexico's now-private phone giant. Since its privatization in 1990, it has maintained dominance in certain competitive areas and made a $10 billion investment to create a modern digital network. But its weaknesses—marketing and an abysmal image—are not normally associated with companies that have gone private. Telmex's weaknesses have lingered because the company has been slow to take its new and old competitors seriously. Further affecting its reputation is that the company still has not lived down its record of dismal service before privatization. In mid-1996, Telmex lost 40 percent of its market share when it lost its near stranglehold on the long-distance market. Telmex's managers can only hope, albeit nervously, that the total market will ultimately expand to cover their initial loss. Shareholders, on the other hand, can only hope that managers go the way of their once-held monopoly.

European policymakers have ambitious plans to privatize, and governments worldwide can be expected to work hard to keep finding buyers. Even regimes that have been cool toward market economics will follow suit. Sweden's Social Democrats plan to sell as much as 75 percent ($2 billion) of Nordbanken, the country's fourth largest bank. Spain's socialist leaders, who have heretofore sold off assets in a slow trickle, are at least internally debating the merits of a broad privatization plan. And after the Netherlands completes the sale of its telecom system this year, its next move will be to privatize the railways.

The fundamental problem with privatization, then, is that its speed and progress lie at the mercy of finance and politics. In Europe, investors are used to buying bonds of indebtedness in companies, not shares of equity. In fact, as European markets opened up

The Netherlands' move to privatize its railway is another way in which the country is looking to outside buyers to aid the economy.

and U.S. capital started pouring in, American equity investors found themselves being treated as second class citizens—which consequently created a surge in shareholder activism.

Privatization and Shareholder Rights

Even in emerging Russia, there is the Moscow Committee for Shareholder Rights. When the Derzhava Fund, a Moscow-based investment firm, became fed up with the managers of Yaroslav Rubber Company, a maker of tires and other car and aircraft parts, they were able to join with outside investors and force a change. In the fall of 1994, they installed a new CEO and a team of young financial experts. In three months' time, the company had signed new orders equivalent to all of the previous year's sales. "Things can change fast if you can change the management," says Andrei Volgin, head of the Derzhava Fund and also chairman of the Moscow Committee for Shareholder Rights.

Over the first half of 1995, some 24,000 annual shareholders' meetings were scheduled, many turning into showdowns between former state managers entrenched in their old positions and private investors-turned-activists demanding better performance. Says Dmitri Vasilyev, Deputy Chairman of Russia's new Securities Commission, "Many will lose their posts and be replaced by more qualified people." By one estimate, up to 4,800 CEOs could get the boot along with many directors. Most likely, however, the Russian old guard won't go out quietly. With capitalism still on shaky ground, Russia remains an unlikely battleground for shareholder rights—at least for the near term. And keeping with the fond, old memories of all the trappings of communist power, these managers are going so far as to lobby the government to stall economic reforms. They common-

ly resort to such tactics as wrapping themselves in the flag and claiming that outside investors are only moving in to strip mother Russia of her wealth. Some have even gone so far as to erase the names of outside investors from computerized shareholder lists. But the pro-reform forces led by Premier Victor S. Chernomyrdin seems determined to push for reform at the company level, so shareholders will be allowed to install new managements, and subsidies will eventually be yanked away from failing companies.

Because of privatizations, European governments must in a sense pray that stock sales roll when they offer up a state-owned company. Surely, though, they are aware of the sheer abundance of dollars in the world marketplace. In terms of paper money alone, half of the U.S. currency in circulation is held outside of America. Russia's stock of dollars is thought to run as high as $30 billion (including several billion in counterfeit $100 bills—slowed now by the minting of the new $100 bill). And with American dollars and Japanese yen coursing though the globe for investment opportunities (even after the Mexican peso debacle) those governments were confident enough from mid-1995 through 1996 to have offered a full $30 billion in equities across Europe.

Those with bonds in their blood may be wondering whether privatization in Europe will force them to mutate into equity disciples. So far, modest continental equity markets have hobbled entrepreneurial companies. How, then, can risk-averse investors be made into such stockholders? Look towards the example of the biggest privatizing deal to be done in Germany. Chancellor Helmut Kohl wants his long-awaited sell-off of Deutsche Telekom to produce a "people's stock," to help build a European equity culture. To accomplish this, and to satisfy the risk-averse investor, Kohl intends to break the deal up into bits and pieces.

The effects of privatization will invigorate many struggling societies.

Though possibly the best means towards ultimate privatization, the process moves along slowly. The first 20 percent slice of the blockbuster DT deal was accomplished this year. The shares offered equaled a staggering 7 percent of the total value of the Frankfurt stock exchange's DAX index of 30 blue chips. Due to the immensity of Deutsche Telekom, there is little wonder why Kohl is taking it one step at a time. Other countries are doing the same. Portugal has sold off the first 28 percent of Portugal Telecom to small investors as well as big institutions. It plans a similar sale of the state tobacco company Tabaqueira.

The Effect of Politics on Your Business

Throughout these economic developments, politics are sure to continue to cause big headaches. Extremist parties of the left and right routinely take potshots at centrist privatization plans, as they did when the sale of Italian energy and chemical giant ENI was proposed in 1995. A center-right coalition had hoped to regain power in Italy in 1996. The party was privatization-friendly, but its allies in the far right National Alliance were not. So the center-right lost to the Olive Tree coalition of market-oriented centrists and former Communists who have embraced privatization. Now, the Olive Tree's leader, Romano Prodi, is at battle with leftist opponents of privatization within his own coalition. The hard-line Communist Reconstruction Party, which supported the Olive Tree in the April elections, opposes privatization and is pushing for restoration of the wage indexing that did so much to entrench inflation in the 1970s. Still, Prodi has settled on his first target: the giant state-controlled telecom firm, Stet. His righthand man in the Olive Tree, Communist Party daily paper editor Walter Vetroni, is ambitious to remake the Italian left in the image of the U.S. Democratic Party.

Meanwhile, the British government hoped to privatize British Rail and two nuclear utilities in 1996. But that certainly won't happen if the Labor Party succeeds in pushing out the Conservatives. Constituents of the former are more likely to have blue-collar backgrounds and union ties, and unions fight privatization because of the loss of jobs that are sure to follow.

The People Principle of Privatization

Studies have shown that lost jobs are almost always a casualty of state sell-offs, as profit-driven managements restructure and downsize their companies. In Chapter 2, we saw that although jobs are lost initially, downsizing has a net affect of creating a better trained workforce and healthier, more stockholder-friendly companies. However, unions still have a reason to cry foul, as in the near-term jobs are cut. And with huge state-run corporations, there is often the added strain of voter empathy. Private companies do not need to win public votes, though they had better win the hearts of shareholders—as we've seen with several recent European shareholder victories.

Don't think this means that labor is going to run for the hills. Strikes and worker discord can easily abort the privatization process. When private-bound Deutsche Telecom laid off a total of 14,000 workers over a period of two years, labor forces shut it down. Finally, share swaps between state-owned companies of different countries were required to get the ball rolling.

This combustible mix of unions and investors is possibly the biggest deterrent to swift privatizations in countries where the government is eager to shed assets. Two deals were recently postponed in Britain—a country considered a trailblazer in the game—due to the clash of capital and labor. In April, 1995, after two British electric utilities were sold, regulators cut rates, which dug into profits and outraged investors. To add insult to injury, the common practice of directors voting themselves fat pay hikes directly after privatization has done little to extinguish the anger of an enraged public. Such divisive measures are causing both the pro and con side of the privatization argument to take their time with both the decision-making and the process. Amid fears of being ripped off, people tend to move forward cautiously.

Another source of delay is that cautious governments try to wait and let deals go through in other countries before their own. Why throw yourself under the microscope if there's a chance to work outside of an unforgiving spotlight? That may well be the case with the German airline Lufthansa. Bonn has only tentative plans to sell its final 36 percent stake in the carrier by 1997—after beginning the process years earlier. By going slowly, in almost unnoticeable increments, a government can let swifter and bloodier privatizations in other countries like Britain carry the news. All it needs to do is hide behind the "length of the deal" and chalk up any disgruntlement brought on by the restructuring of its assets to "normal market conditions."

European investors should ask how divested companies have performed on the whole. The answer is that it may be too early to tell—at least for the latest round of European sell-offs. As of July, 1995, all but one of the six companies France had privatized beginning in early 1994 were trading at, or below, their offering prices. But that would seem largely attributable to Europe's weak recovery. Globally, a strong and affirmative consensus has developed for the continuation of foreign investment. A recent survey by Greenwich, Connecticut-based consulting firm Greenwich Associates found that of 1,620 U.S. pension funds managing $2.7 billion in assets, 65 percent already invest abroad—and 28 percent more plan to do so shortly. Seventeen percent of these funds are also playing the emerging markets and are sticking by their investments despite 1994's global downtrend.

When performance averages are considered, there are no surprises in their philosophies. Global investing has paid off for them, and others, through all the panics, uncertainties and calamities they've encountered. Stamford, Connecticut-based financial consulting firm InterSec Research Corp. estimates that U.S. pension funds earned a compounded annual return of 18.2 percent on overseas investments over the past 10 years. That's nearly four percentage points greater than what the funds would have earned by investing in the mainly domestic stocks that make up *Standard & Poor's* 500-stock average. "U.S. investors are finally convinced that 'international' is something that belongs in their portfolios," says InterSec Director James A. Diack.

However, massive flows of cross-border capital can cause upsets, as the turbulence in the markets of 1994 demonstrated. During this same period, the federal government hiked interest rates to ward off inflation, and many investors shifted their capital back to U.S. shores to take advantage of the higher yields. This, coupled with the Mexican economic debacle—and the shivers it sent through Latin America, Eastern Europe, and Asia—was enough to make the more timid think twice before shipping their money overseas again. But markets have rebounded, and U.S. overseas investments have risen. 1995's marker of $330 billion was up nearly $100 billion from 1994's $233 billion. Still, that is short of 1993's $437 billion, but most money watchers feel that the upcoming years after will challenge 1993's record —especially with the coming raft of privatizations in Brazil, a railroad sale in Canada, and several more European properties coming up for sale.

France also presents a good example of the complex atmosphere of pri-

vatization. For two years it had been Europe's top privatizer, but as the May, 1995 presidential elections approach-ed, nearly all deals were halted. By mid-1996, the government was strapped for cash to cut deficits. Concurrent and heavy spending to create jobs wasn't helping. So the French government jumped back into the privatization game and offered investors $2 billion worth of stock in Usinor Sacilor—Europe's biggest steelmaker, and conservative President Jacques Chirac's flagship for the privatization campaign he wants France to undertake. Market reception to the deal was good too, mainly because the company had just broken into the black. But this was hardly a success that will be easily repeated. Despite the French government's efforts, it is unlikely that sales in companies slated for privatization over the near-term can be accelerated. The reasons are that the unions are active, the franc's future is cloudy, and the remaining firms to be sold are less appealing than Usinor.

In the East, India presents an intriguing example of a promising but troublesome climate for privatization. India is the world's largest democracy, yet it is one of the world's poorest countries—coupled with a population that could exceed China's in the next century. With such pressures looming, India could sorely use the privatization of state-held enterprises. Indeed, privatization was a central part of the five-year reform plan launched by Prime Minister P.V.N. Rao in 1991. About 200 of the country's 220 centrally owned companies are chronic money-losers, and the situation is even worse for companies owned by individual states. The states' habit of heavy borrowing from the central government helped to drive up short-term interest rates, throughout the economy, to 20 percent in 1996, even as the government attacked inflation. Interest payments now consume at least half of government revenues. Clearly, radical

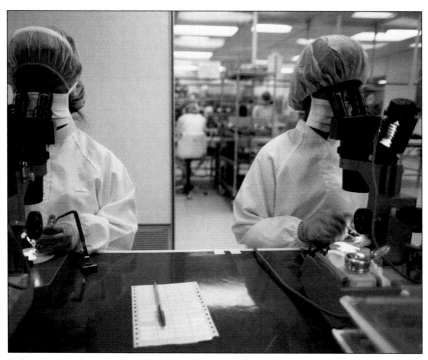

India is a promising arena for privatization.

privatization would free up massive re-sources for social spending and infra-structure improvements, but India continues to ramble along at a pace not conducive to these types of changes. The government has vowed to keep at least 51 percent ownership of state companies precisely because over 190 million Indians live below the poverty line. Recall the problems encountered by the British government when work-ers—who also vote—balked at the sale of state assets. The same scenario is playing out in India, where the labor force is well aware of the cost-cutting measures that privatization would bring to once secure workplaces. Unfortunately, Indian politicians have to go where the votes are, which is often a matter of playing to labor's fears in an economy where millions are already forced to get by on less than $9 per month. "There is a big fear that the country is being sold too cheaply," says Mrityunjay Athreya, a consultant in New Delhi.

Privatization in India would require a political consensus of a sort almost unknown in the West. Thus, the process plods along in fits and starts while large-scale political foment continues, especially since the dethroning of the Congress Party. In place now—since the elections of mid-1996—is the most frail of coalition governments. But the good news is that no political party is even entertaining the idea of turning back the reforms that have already taken place. Feeling some assurance, many investors are taking the view that India remains promising no matter how glacial its rate of change. Some portfolio investors are even bullish on India, noting that foreigners poured $1.2 billion into the long-depressed Bombay exchange in the first half of 1996. That's almost as much as in all of 1995. As a result, the market has risen more than 25 percent since the beginning of this year. The risk is that the promising reforms already in place will get stuck halfway, just as global competition from other privatizing countries gets stronger. It is also likely that privatization will continue to be postponed, which constitutes an object lesson for those who would invest in state companies. However slow or fast a country's privatization, investors are usually better off moving fast in order to avoid finding more trouble ahead. Should you deem India's pace to be too slow, you may just find happier hunting elsewhere.

Looking south, consider the privatization case of YPF's Lujan de Cuyo refinery in the Andean foothills of western Argentina. In 1990 when it was state-owned, the staff numbered 700 employees. Now that YPF is in private hands, the refinery has only 49 employees. Says refinery manager Luis Angel Castillo, "If everything is going well, the place runs itself from the control room. The fewer people, the better."

Efficiency is the mantra of private YPF these days. Attempting to transform itself from elephant to gazelle, it cut its overall workforce to 6,750 from 51,000. And market share has not suffered—YPF still controls half of Argentina's oil market. It is also now the most public relations-conscious company in the country, after years of having the reputation of being aloof and arrogant. Shiny new outlets selling only environmentally friendly unleaded gasoline corroborate the evidence of a company making money. Red ink was the norm throughout the 1980s under state ownership, but in the first half of 1995, two years after YPF went private, solid management netted $401 million.

Even with these advances, the company continues to look for respect on the floor of the New York Stock Exchange. Its shares have languished since its $3 billion initial public offering in 1993, even though Americans and other foreign investors own half of YPF's stock. "This is one of the cheapest integrated oil companies in the world," says James A. Shore, portfolio manager for San Diego-based Brandes Investment Partners Inc., whose firm has snapped up 3.5 million YPF shares. Merrill Lynch & Co. First VP, Constantine D. Fliakos, figures the company is trading at half the value of its net assets. Its reserves,

amounting to 1 billion barrels of crude oil and 8.5 trillion cubic feet of gas, alone may be worth $29 per American Depository Receipt. So why the lack of respect? The answer is jitters, another overseas fact of life, particularly with privatizations in unsettled economies or regions.

Since the Mexican collapse, Argentina and other Latin markets have been forced to endure the resultant squeeze. Moreover, YPF turned controversial when it purchased Maxus Energy Corp., an indebted Texas oil and gas producer. In demonstrating that privatization is a two-way street, YPF drew the ire of some U.S. money managers who became critical of the company for going global. Some blame it on YPF's failure to properly massage foreign stockholders. But new CEO Nells Leon says, "They're not used to an emerging market company buying a U.S. company." Some even point to the recent death of YPF's previous and dynamic CEO, Jose A. Estenssoro, citing it as a factor in the suppressed price. Whatever the truth, the stock still isn't moving. Are there any lessons to be learned here? Yes: Privatizations can quickly turn a company around, but due to factors far beyond their control, stockholders may be in for a long, detour-filled ride to increased stock prices and value, due to factors beyond their control. Thai auto consultant Michael Dunne advised newcomers to hang in there for the long haul. Though he was speaking about foreign companies entering the labor market, his words apply equally well to foreign investment in privatizations.

Other countries where privatization is yielding results include, but are not limited to, Russia, South Korea, South Africa, Brazil, and even Mexico. "To invest in an emerging economy and have all the headaches that go with it, I should see substantial capital gains potential," says independent money manager Marc Faber. "Otherwise it's hardly worth it." To Faber, that means taking a flyer on oil and gas stocks in Russia. "If

Privatization is yielding results in countries such as South Korea.

Russia can move successfully to a Western capitalist society," he predicts, "its shares could be mind boggling."

Asian hands are looking to South Korea, where recent privatizations, declining interest rates, cooling inflation, and rapid earnings growth are giving equities a lift. While Asia remains the world's growth machine, some pros believe that South Africa has equal potential. Emerging from years of apartheid and worldwide ignominy, the heavily industrialized country is positioning itself to become the commercial hub of the vast area south of the Sahara. In Mexico, the Zedillo government has struggled to set things right after the crash. The cost has been high, but Mexico's trade balance is in the black, the peso appears stable, and the solvency crisis that triggered the 1994 meltdown has evaporated—with the help of U.S. aid. The government has even returned to international capital markets by selling off $2.1 billion in debt in the summer of 1995. Brazilian President Fernando Henrique Cardosa's efforts to turn the economy away from consumption and toward privatizations and investment-led growth has Latin American investors taking heart. Some think a big winner in the Brazilian economy could be the state-controlled Companhia Vale do Rio Doce, the world's largest producer of iron ore. Cardosa wants to sell the behemoth for $9 billion this year. One money manager raves about Brazil, citing that it is a country that has survived an inflation rate of 5,000 percent. High marks are also given to Brazil's business management. As a result of the aforementioned activity, world watchers believe that enormous levels of profitability are possible in Latin and South America.

The bad news is that regardless of where you invest your capital or time, some deals won't be profitable. Beware of all the euphoric forecasts besieging you in the media—no one's going to fault you for a healthy level of skepticism. Learn from the lessons of others, as documented in this chapter. Study the area you intend to pursue, then study it again. Take into consideration how stable the politics in a particular region are. Look into how well policy-makers are managing currencies and economies. Be prepared to wait out periods of non-existent returns on under-performing assets. And always remember that like any worthwhile venture, moving into foreign markets is not without its risks.

Of course, be equally aware of risk's flipside—rewards. They travel as a couple, and in the emerging markets, and the opportunities brought on by privatizations, you'll have plenty of chances to meet up with both of them. Subject the facts and figures to microscopic-like

scrutiny, and the risks you take will be calculated more heavily in your favor. Going global is helping a lot of people and companies meet their targeted rates of growth. Due to the complex factors involved in privatization and government divestment of assets, sometimes even the most well-advised investors may, at times, find themselves jumping over unexpected hurdles. By careful surveying opening markets, and anticipating possible problems prior to entry, the flexible and savvy businessperson is well-positioned for global growth.

Chapter 4

Piracy, Copyrights, and Your Recourse Options

The Mouse is roaring through China. Books are being knocked off, software is being pirated, and video-cassettes are at the heart of the black market. One of the prime targets of counterfeiters is the Walt Disney Company. Disney was riled when it found taped copies of its hit movie, *The Lion King,* on sale in Beijing before the official videotape release date. Always a staunch protector of its intellectual property, the company has decided to get tough.

Recently, Disney and other American businesses, including Harcourt Brace, Lotus Development, Autodesk, and Microsoft began testing the waters of China's fledgling legal copyright protections system. Together, as of early 1995, the companies have filed as many as 25 copyright infringement lawsuits in China's three-year-old Intellectual Property Tribunal of the Beijing Intermediate People's Court. Several more lawsuits are planned. And though the companies expect little meaningful relief to come their way as a result of their legal offensive, they say the move represents an important step outside of diplomatic channels toward deterring piracy. "We never had

Copyright infringement lawsuits have "crawled along at a snail's pace," in China's People's Court.

any illusions that if we spent zillions of dollars bringing cases, we could stop the piracy," says Eric H. Smith, president of the Washington-based International Intellectual Property Alliance (IIPA). "But part of our strategy is to test the system."

At first, results from the legal strategy were promising. In June of 1994, after a flurry of lawsuits, 22 Beijing officials and U.S. company representatives raided six major computer software dealers to seize evidence. Since then, the cases have "crawled along at a snail's pace," according to Valeria Colbourn, Microsoft's Hong Kong-based attorney. While the new People's Court has ruled in favor of Disney in a case where two children's publishing companies had illegally sold magazines featuring Disney characters, the issue of monetary damages has yet to be resolved. Microsoft has also prevailed with its trademark-infringement case. Shenzhen Reflective Materials Institute, an industrial lab at state-run Shenzhen University, was churning out counterfeit holographs like those the software

giant affixes to its program packages. However, vindication in the People's Court was a merely symbolic victory that amounted only to a paltry $2,600 in compensation, even though Microsoft says it has lost $26 million in sales of counterfeit software so far.

The U.S./China Trade Relations Cycle

While Chinese TV programs show officials destroying illegal knock-offs of U.S. products, and reports circulate that some counterfeiters have been executed, U.S. exporters remain dubious about the extent of China's recent crackdown on counterfeiters. "Everyone operating in China has a baseline fear that once the technology and management know-how are transferred, the Chinese will try to squeeze you out," says Richard A. Brescher, an official with the U.S.-China Business Council in Washington, D.C. Considering that

China's trade surplus with the U.S. hit a record $40 billion in 1995 (and is well on the way to surpassing Japan's $66 billion surplus by the end of the decade), many are fuming. A February 20, 1995 *BusinessWeek* editorial elaborates: "Now is the perfect time for Washington to make it clear that the U.S. and the global trading system are open to only those who play by the rules. Running 29 factories that counterfeit American software and videodisks is simply not acceptable in a trading partner. It is more than a matter of knocking off copies of *The Lion King*. The intellectual-property conflict revolves around Chinese piracy of U.S. technology and management know-how on a broad scale. After Chrysler Corp. invested millions of dollars in China to build Jeeps, it discovered to its horror that the Chinese were knocking them off—with no apology." Thus, the ostensibly profitable trade relationship the U.S. maintains with China remains a highly controversial one.

Some would go on to argue that U.S. Trade Representative Mickey Kantor should make the abolishment of counterfeiting and the trade deficit a prerequisite before China is granted permission to join the World Trade Organization. But forcing the issue of business ethics and threatening to impose punitive tariffs on Chinese exports to America could result in a setback to politically based goals. Of course, there is also the possibility of China's retaliation. Many investors would rather not take the chance that China might retaliate by imposing hurtful trade restrictions and a suspension of talks with possible U.S. joint venturers.

The question being commonly asked now is: Is this a cost of setting up business in an emerging market or is it just plain lawlessness? Considering that China's mega-economy is likely to equal or exceed the U.S. economy in the coming few decades, it may be difficult to come up with an answer that pleases all of the concerned parties. Obviously, the stakes for U.S. businesses are enormous, as China's sheer size and potential make it impossible to ignore as a key player. "Any international company that's not planning to do something in China is probably missing a bet," says J. Tracy O'Rourke, CEO of Varian Associates Inc., a California-based manufacturer of medical equipment. "It's like the frontier of days past."

Even with the pitfalls of piracy in China, it remains a land offering incredible opportunities to traders in software and entertainment. Likely, the crackdown on counterfeiters will continue beyond what some today criticize as lip service, as pressure on the Chinese government increases. Already, some executives seem pleased with steps taken to confiscate or halt the back-alley production of low-priced dubs and pirated CD-ROMS. Since the accord was struck between the U.S. and China in February 1995, authorities finished out the year by conducting 3,000 raids in which millions of illicit items were confiscated. But with profit margins running as high as 40 percent, dealers are continuously lured onto the streets. One group argues that the anti-counterfeiting battle's fundamental weakness is that it lacks enforcability. Others claim the struggle comes down to a battle of wills. Some charge that it is both, and that the Chinese have responded far too slowly. But the fact remains that the legislation of recent years has had enough impact so that exporters are better off now than they were five years ago.

Software Piracy Worldwide

By no means is China the only offender. The Software Publishers Association estimates that the worldwide value of plundered software totals at least $16 billion annually. And despite all

Eastern Europe is facing down software pirates—with mixed results.

the adverse publicity, China is only part of the problem. In Europe alone, the London-based Business Software Alliance estimates that piracy throughout Europe cost the industry about $6 billion in 1994, up 22 percent from 1993 (legitimate sales amounted to $10.5 billion in 1994). This comes despite a widespread push to curb the problem. In fact, software piracy rates actually fell in most Western European countries.

How is it, then, that piracy rates continue to climb? The answer lies in Eastern Europe, a software pirate's paradise. Despite crackdowns, illegally produced software accounted for more than 90 percent of the software in use in the Eastern European market in 1994. In Turkey and parts of the former Soviet Union, piracy rates accounted for a staggering 97 percent of the entire software market, a loss to legitimate manufacturers of more than $150 million. Other notable offenders include Bulgaria and Romania, with piracy rates of 95 percent and collective losses of $52 million. The Russian Federation alone cost software makers $540

million due to its 94 percent piracy rate. Poland's pirates made off with $201 million, and Hungary and the Czech Republic added about $100 million each to illegitimate sales in the same year.

The thriving black market in Eastern Europe is so bad that some companies, such as Microsoft, have offered to make the pirates official software dealers if they agree to come clean. Oracle Corp. has even considered implementing a sort of amnesty problem. When Oracle began to focus on selling in Central and Eastern European markets in 1990, it found that it already had an installed base numbering in the thousands, even though not a single copy of genuine Oracle software had been sold in those areas. More than 10,000 installed users were found in the former Soviet Union alone. In Bulgaria, Oracle discovered a former state-run agency that had translated its software, repackaged it, and sold it under the name "Cars." Copies were being sold to government agencies, banks, and corporations. While that particular practice has since stopped, the general phenomenon has yet to subside.

"We've had games appear in the Eastern European market that hadn't even been officially released in Europe," said Roger Bennett, director of the European Leisure Software Publishers Association, which represents the computer and video-game business. Mr. Bennett is hoping that the same concerns about piracy being raised in China will eventually take hold in Eastern Europe and promote legislation there as well. "It's just getting through to the powers that be that they should be more concerned," he said. "The problem seems to be getting better," says Debbie Lloyd, regional commercial manager of Oracle East Central Europe, based in Vienna. Lloyd continues: "The question is, what does 'better' really mean?"

Some fault public perception. For years, law-abiding citizens have passed around dog-eared copies of old paperbacks and no one has objected. Charities hold book sales and blank video cassettes are legitimately sold in five- and ten-packs (for illegally recording your favorite programs and movies). Even in Singapore, the most law-abiding of nations (7 armed robberies in 1995 in a population of 3 million), copies of Microsoft Works, a $100 package, sell for $25 on the street. In Bangkok, name the program you want and pirates there will charge you a flat fee of $5 per disk to duplicate it.

Legal Reform— Hope for Future Business?

Sound discouraging? Fortunately, slow, yet positive forces may help to reverse this trend. Several countries are actually doing something about piracy. Spain, Hungary, and Poland have broadened their copyright laws to cover software and have introduced tough new sentences for software pirates. A campaign

in Italy has helped to scale back software piracy from 90 percent in 1990 to 57 percent in 1994. "Even if you bring piracy rates down from 90 percent to 80 percent, you have doubled the size of the [legitimate software] market," argues Allen Dixon of the Business Software Alliance. Mexico is another example of a country determined to combat piracy. Anti-piracy teams from the Attorney General's office have searched the offices of some of the country's largest corporations, resulting in settlements being paid to Apple, Microsoft, Lotus, and WordPerfect.

With such crackdowns in mind, software makers forge optimistically on into new and often lawless markets. And regardless of popular or private opinion, one such market, China, remains a place of boundless promise for the soft-trader. The marketplace consists not only of China's population of more than 1 billion people, but also of the 400 million additional Mandarin-speaking inhabitants of Malaysia, Indonesia, and Singapore. And as never before, its citizens are beginning to challenge a system that has grown increasingly permissive over the years.

Entertainment and Business—a Perfect Global Pairing

On a Sunday night in early 1996, 3,000 students at the Beijing University of Science and Technology listened raptly to six bands playing forbidden Chinese equivalents of rock, grunge, and heavy metal music. The acts included He Yong and Dou Wei, two of China's hottest stars. Tickets to the forbidden concert were never issued or sold, and neither the bands nor the music company backing them made any money. But the concert was a significant happening, and not simply because it wasn't broken up by law enforcement. As it would have in free countries, the event helped the bands sell hundreds of tapes and CDs by word-of-mouth. That bolstered the reputation of Taiwan's Rock Records, an independent label promoting local talent—and local talent in that marketplace means a potential customer base of several hundred million. That means that Rock Records' ascension may someday enable it to take on big, worldwide names like Polygram and Sony.

A new global frontier is defining the type of software produced and is affecting the music scene, movies, and other types of entertainment. The once-vaunted demand for American entertainment has receded, and new entertainment hubs are springing up in an expanding number of foreign countries. Hip or high standards are no longer set by U.S. or British megastars, be they Michael Jackson, the Rolling Stones, Tom Cruise or, for that matter, Microsoft. Today, the action has shifted to locales far afield, where rela-

tively indigenous soft products are gaining popularity. And although America may be partially losing its foothold as the center of the entertainment world, this trend could definitely bode well for the globally minded entrepreneur. Globally, stirrings of a certain modest following are based on such heady principles as nationalism and provincialism. This represents quite a transformation in the entertainment and software industries. Think back to the Bombay, India, example in Chapter 1, where local film producers are introducing audiences to special effects-driven movies fashioned after megahits like *Speed* and *Jurassic Park*. Local sensibilities are being infused into the productions in a shrewd move that may very well soften demand for subsequent U.S. blockbusters. After all, why watch another country's films when yours offer the same production values—and themes that strike closer to home?

Key foreign markets, such as Brazil, are growing rapidly—particularly in nationalist areas such as music.

It's no wonder, then, that the big growth is now expected to be in "local repertoire," a phenomenon that is anticipated to vault to prominence in our growing "global village"—a term coined by trend forecaster Marshall McLuhan 30 years ago. While the U.S. music market remained flat in 1995, key foreign markets, including Brazil, Indonesia, Poland, South Africa, Hong Kong, and Japan, grew at healthy clips of anywhere between 20 percent to 55 percent in annual sales. Although a music market like Brazil's is, in absolute terms, only a tenth the size of Japan's, even that ratio was unfathomable just two years ago. What explains such a sudden growth spurt? These countries aren't abruptly awakening to their local talent. Rather, the truth is that young people from Warsaw to Beijing are enjoying the rising disposable income that typified American baby boomers in the 1970s and '80s—albeit without the boomers' current responsibilities to professions and families.

The music-buying youth of Beijing or Belgrade will still line up to buy the latest hits from the likes of Bon Jovi or Michael Bolton, but they increasingly want to hear stars who speak their own language or reflect their own culture. The lifestyle of someone like Madonna is too far removed from that of an engineering student in Beijing. But that's not the case with Dou Wei, whose albums sell to domestic Chinese, to large numbers of transplanted Chinese abroad, and to other customers worldwide. Italy's Laura Pausini has swept Europe, and now, with a Spanish-language record, is a hit in Latin America as well. Dadawa, a Chinese star getting a global push from Warner Music, accomplished a successful European tour in 1995. Hong Kong singer Jacky Cheung recently made Polygram's Top 10 roster, the first Asian to do so.

Not surprisingly, prospectors from the biggest media and software conglomerates are routinely scouring the likes of Latin coffeehouses, Asian karaoke clubs, and school computer and dance clubs in central Europe. They search for acts and products that can make it big in their native lands and then make it globally—perhaps to a lesser extent than a traditional music superstar or video blockbuster, but to a greater extent than ever before. Furthermore, with the increasing revenues generated from homespun acts, governments are becoming more protective of those making legitimate sales. If China, for example, is finally taking U.S. complaints over piracy seriously, it is probably even more likely that it will listen to its native Chinese businesspeople complain over the very same issue. Businesses in these sectors will simply not be able to make money if they are competing against counterfeited products.

Logistical Considerations Overseas

The manufacturer or supplier looking abroad should be prepared to encounter tight government controls and rampant piracy in major markets like India and Thailand as well. Investing in an entertainment or software business in those countries will be fraught with risk. It wasn't too long ago that exporting videos, records, or software copies involved nothing more inspired than spending a little extra on overhead. Now, a target country must first be scouted for its indigenous products—from its pop stars to its best-selling, off-the-shelf business software.

Global investors are also advised to expect a struggle when dealing with the logistics of a major overseas promotion, as well as with manufacturing and distribution. However, the record growth in overseas markets (recall the 20 percent to 55 percent growth in select music markets), is causing companies

With a new middle-class emerging, products such as CD-ROMS are expected to find new audiences.

to decide in favor of doing the additional work associated with a tailor-made product. After all, it's not very likely that sales were effortlessly handed to these same companies domestically. Moreover, a local soft product may still make far less money globally than its U.S. counterpart, but if it finds wide popularity or sales across a region, it will give global competitors a scare—particularly if the product is promoted by a joint venture with a suitable foreign distributor. It is also important to consider the size of "local" markets, which on a global scale can exceed the size of many entire countries. Markets such as India or China each exceed the size, in terms of population, of the entire English speaking world. Remember, "local" is a relative term.

Not surprisingly, in a variety of software and entertainment industries, powerful players are consolidating to facilitate takeovers. Liquor giant Seagram recently acquired music and film giant MCA. Steven Spielberg's DreamWorks SKG, Sumner Redstone's Viacom, Inc., Rupert Murdoch's News Corp., and Michael D. Eisner's Walt Disney Co. are all eagerly sifting through worldwide software and entertainment opportunities. Several have already entered the marketplace with products, and a few, including a partnership between DreamWorks SKG and Microsoft, are poised to do so.

Of course, regional entertainment companies, often run by streetwise local entrepreneurs, are predictably savvier about spotting new opportunities and talent in their own backyards than are the giants. That's how in 16 years, Rock Records has built itself into eastern Asia's largest independent record label, with 50 Chinese-language artists, including the region's most popular stars. Sales were an estimated $85 million in 1995—an amount equal to all music sales that year in South Africa, a mature Commonwealth market.

South Korea and Poland will also become fertile markets now that their governments are demonstrating intolerance of illegal sales, and youth buying power has increased. Meanwhile, half a world away, Latin American countries have resolutely worked to stabilize their economies. Brazil and Mexico, in particular, are taking their places among the top ten soft markets in the world. It will be years however, before Russia's government controls are rolled back and piracy is curtailed.

Modern Media-based Technology Sparks New Business

Governmental cooperation, the most difficult aspect of policing, seems to have been conquered. Regardless of illegal activities, a new middle-class is mushrooming in locales as diverse as Moscow, Prague, and Mexico City. Residents hunger for a mix of local, regional, and foreign software, CD-ROMs, music CDs, and videos. It's not hard to envision that small "soft-firms," as well as large, established conglomerates, will be striving to satisfy them in the 1990s and beyond by means of imports, joint ventures, subsidies, licensing agreements, or otherwise.

Looming middle-class audiences abroad are likewise spurring investment in new technical delivery systems. Just because a country's broadcast audience is highly educated and sophisticated, and its culture broadly developed, doesn't mean that its media infrastructure has kept up. In at least a few countries, technology needs an overhaul, and U.S. service companies are clamoring to get in. An example could be found in Japan, where traditional broadcasting is of the highest technical caliber. However, the nation has lagged behind the West in obtaining newer services such as cable and satellite broadcasting. Currently, Japanese TV audiences have only 12 channels available to them on regular analog TV. This doesn't mean that finally, the thickened doors of Japanese trade are freely swinging open to Westerners. But

among those countries with lagging services, there is a pervasive need for Western technology and support.

Because improving delivery systems is hardly a social matter, fewer hackles are being raised than would be in the case of programming or content issues. Therefore, foreign governments are usually very accommodating. For example, the huge task of "wiring China"—to be partly subbed out to overseas companies—is a lot more palatable to Chinese leaders than importing or permitting Western-style live rock music. Consequently, more doors are opening to foreigners providing such services than would be the case with those wishing to import soft product that the government may deem unsuitable for its people.

One company that wasted no time capitalizing on the potentially vast demand for entertainment technology abroad is Rupert Murdoch's Sydney-based News Corp., which over the last several years has waged an aggressive campaign to expand its global reach by creating satellite TV ventures throughout the world. Attempting to duplicate the success of its BSkyB satellite business in Britain, News Corp. has launched similar ventures in Japan, Latin America, Europe, the U.S., and China. In April, 1996, Murdoch's Hong Kong-based StarTV initiated a new era of foreign broadcasting in Japan with the launch of a 24-hour all-digital channel called StarPlus. The channel broadcasts all programming in Japanese, or with Japanese subtitles, and plans to expand to six channels by the second quarter of 1998. Within the same period, Murdoch plans to launch a 100-channel satellite TV service, to be called JSkyB. Additionally, a pay-per-view movie channel, dubbed Star Movies, began broadcasting in December, 1996.

News Corp.'s strong push in Japan was prompted by the imminent entry of other digital systems there, such as Hughes Electronics' DirecTV and PerfectTV, run by a group of Japanese

Latin America is a hot new market for products such as cable television and digital TV.

companies. Unlike the Chinese, the Japanese are receptive to a wide range of native-language programming. That makes digital satellite TV hot, because traditionally, satellite operators have recognized the need to provide native-language programming far more so than cable operators. Satellite TV also holds the promise of "leapfrogging" cable in those countries where cable's installed-base-per-capita is still negligible. In addition to operating its satellite venture, News Corp. intends to become a wholesale supplier of programming to Japanese cable. The company, which owns 20th Century Fox's film library, shouldn't find that particular venture too difficult.

Latin America is also shaping up as a major playing field for digital TV, which, like cable, is virtually unknown there. Two competing ventures, Sky Latin America and Galaxy Latin America, are preparing to beam satellite TV across the continent, establishing broadcast centers in seven cities, from Long Beach, California, in the north to Sao Paulo, Brazil, in the south. The

centers will uplink TV programs to a satellite that will beam them back down to a potential audience of 450 million people. Together the two players will have invested more than $1 billion in their respective ventures by 1998, a figure that translates into more than $2.33 per inhabitant and $40 per forecasted eventual subscriber.

Legal Issues— What the Future Holds

As entertainment and the information media become globally standardized, experts predict that there will be a far greater emphasis on the protection of intellectual property rights abroad, not less. The evolution of less-developed countries in this area will proceed at different rates, but along pretty much the same continuum, according to Paul Oliva, executive director of Bay Trade in San Francisco. When a less-developed country fully enters the media

Piracy was a big problem in Taiwan before the government implemented strict self-monitoring.

arena, its interest in bona fide intellectual protections will increase as it seeks to protect its own.

India is a case in point. It has long been a key proponent of no patent protection on pharmaceuticals, because it wants to provide the lowest cost to its enormous population. But India must inevitably rethink this position as it continues to develop its own computer, software, and motion picture industries. What incentive is there for an Indian firm to invest any money in R&D when it knows that the Indian government isn't going to protect it? Imagine your government looking the other way while your innovative product is counterfeited next door. You could be smart, as Ray Ban was when it offered a lower-priced class of sunglasses to compete directly with counterfeiters. Or you could stop production altogether and go home. Most likely, however you won't have to exercise this option. Worldwide, governments are looking towards the success of countries that have taken on the pirates within, and following their examples.

Different countries will enter the high-tech development cycle in very different stages and with different timing. The Southeast Asian economies are already considerably further along than India in protecting intellectual rights. But lagging behind India are South America, Eastern Europe, and Africa. Taiwan is a good case study. Early on, Taiwan was a counterfeiting center. Then, the Taiwanese government got serious, gathering up fake Rolex watches and jailing pirates. The resulting security makes opening markets more attractive. Now, companies based there produce state-of-the-art products that Taiwan benefits from in employment and taxation.

Evidence increasingly points to a potential, if limited, global market for almost any entertainment or information product. Software of all types, especially multimedia CD-ROMs, have evolved from business tools to broad means of communication, just like records or videos. And demand for these products will continue to grow as the world evolves into a global village.

Factor in worldwide wage increases, especially among the young, and you'll see a combustible rate of growth in the entertainment sector. But take note of piracy, and particularly the culture buying into it. In China, where consumer money has always been tight and will remain so for some time, the budgeted computer user is going to be strongly tempted to purchase Windows 95 off the street for $4.00, rather than relinquish a month's wages for the legitimate product.

The one hindrance to software sales, then, is the sheer cost of purchasing the real thing. Until smaller CD formats become available, per-unit production costs decrease, and the market shifts altogether from discs to on-demand downloads, demand could suffer. Generally, when an environment exists that too many find too expensive, innovators will move in and product prices will fall. Often these innovators end up owning the market. But with software

remaining a big-ticket item, outpricing the most expensive books by a factor of 50 percent, there is some distance yet to travel, especially in emerging markets where the population is still getting by on the barest of necessities.

The evidence worldwide suggests that most countries will begin or continue to fight pirating, and as the precedent of intolerance is set, fewer markets will be able to successfully move vast quantities of counterfeited products. If profit margins are free from the cancer of piracy, consumers will not only benefit from a better quality of goods, but from reduced product costs. Competition will also be more robust in a secured economy, as exporters and local entrepreneurs move in to establish new markets. The benefits will be felt right down the line, and apparently, the world is becoming aware of this fact as country after country begins to honor and respect each others patents, trademarks, and copyrights.

Chapter 5

Workplace Diversity:
A Key to Success

As companies go global, they will become more savvy in conducting their global affairs by using ethnically diverse managers, enterprise-wide computing systems, and sophisticated communications technology. The late Secretary of Commerce Ron Brown said: "Successful businesses will be using their people of ethnic and cultural diversity to broaden their own marketing and product development workforces. They will also use advanced communications to get a competitive edge in foreign markets." What Secre-

tary Brown suggested was that management could better position itself by seeking and hiring executives from the particular country in which their company intended to operate. Of course, the motivations for drawing on foreign-born talent are usually not as high-minded as they are pragmatic. Foreigners speak the language, understand the culture, know the territory, and will seek out what's best in that country for the product or service they're pushing. The benefits are obvious and business has noticed. There is a far greater awareness that companies

Local executives will be heavily recruited to provide companies with an insider's perspective.

are unlikely to succeed in places such as India and China without Indian and Chinese executives.

Global-minded companies are now taking pains to ensure that their executive recruitment efforts are directed at countries and cultures within which they operate. There is also an effort being made to select only those managers that feel a union with the company and share its goals. In other words, companies want their foreign and domestic workers to be happy. One example of corporate efforts is a plan that has been implemented by AT&T. There, a program was launched to bring young foreign-born managers around the world to the U.S. for three-month to two-year periods. On these tours, the foreigners were introduced to company practices that are independently recognized as some of the most efficient in the world. Once sent home, the managers are expected to introduce the corporate culture to district offices in a manner that also accounts for local customs. Just as important, they have been versed on all pertinent operations within the compa-

ny. In this way, the managers have been made a part of the team. Gone are the days when foreign branch offices and subsidiaries were overlooked, disregarded, and forgotten.

More and more companies will be searching the world for executives, and an increasing number of executives will be called upon to bring a global perspective to their jobs, especially in areas of MIS (management information systems) and operations. The problem lies in locating and enticing the local talent. Headhunting is one common method, but smaller companies can also develop relationships with large multinationals and utilize their foreign distributor contacts to find the best-suited and most employable executives. Trade fairs and associations will offer recruiters more opportunities to make contacts abroad—who might in turn provide references for experienced, qualified personnel. In addition, the need for companies to extend their reach throughout previously untapped areas means that more informal networking is sure to enjoy a widespread increase as well. How easily businesses will translate this method of recruitment into material results will clearly vary from industry to industry. The one obvious point shared by all industries, though, is that the demand for foreign managers exists and is sure to grow several-fold.

Recipes For Global Success

The winners of the global profit derbies of the 1990s—characterized by unprecedented "survival of the fittest" struggles—will manage their far-flung operations by relying on Western-style accounting practices, Japanese-style teamwork, and advanced communications technology. At Whirlpool, the CEO starts his day at 7:00 a.m. in a specially equipped conference room at the company's headquarters. There, he talks to his managers in Asia, reviewing sales figures and production glitches, and gossiping about GE Appliances, their biggest competitor. The CEO then spends until noon following the sun across the globe, making conference calls and holding videoconferences with aides in Europe and the Americas. The talks allow him and his foreign managers to make immediate and thoroughly discussed adjustments in operations. In particular, these advanced communication networks ensure that customer complaints are never more than seven days from the CEO's attention. Whirlpool has shrunk the distance between headquarters and district offices and plants with such a hands-on approach. The mammoth strides in cheap, easily accessible communications are bringing overseas operations into the sphere of top management. District managers need no longer feel intimidated by the thousands of miles that separate them from their superiors.

Global executives nowadays are managing nothing less than a revolution

in doing business. They're struggling to stay on top of markets from Latin America to Russia to Thailand. Compounding their efforts is the fact that the markets they've entered are leaping ahead in growth and sophistication. The new business arena is a far cry from the multidivision corporations that became the standard in the 1950s, and the 21st century world of business is rapidly shaping up as a place where boundaries are even less important than they are today. Breakthroughs in biotechnology and digital electronics issue suddenly and unexpectedly from such diverse places as Israel, Malaysia, China, and Latin America. Business evolution is occurring, as new life is being breathed into supposedly mature industries (such as appliance manufacturing and power plant construction) by the demands of the burgeoning middle classes and their governments. Several of the emerging countries are about to enter phases in their histories similar to our public works projects during the Roosevelt, Truman, and Eisenhower administrations. Growth won't be tied solely to the building or updating of the infrastructure—it will extend to include the revamping of decades old policies and the building of the information superhighway—a bit more complicated and capital intensive than our undertakings in the early decades of this century.

Worldwide Experience Heightens Global Competition

One of the outcomes of this surge in growth and development is that technical and managerial know-how will jump continents to new players in Asia and Latin America. And for those corporations that have been in the game for some time, there will be a greater

Competition for executive positions is expected to grow as workers begin to realize their value in the global marketplace.

potential for expansionism, as national protectionism becomes more widely regarded as fiscally incorrect. CEOs will go on the offense to steal a rival's markets while simultaneously playing defense against the likes of, for example, Finnish electronics maker Nokia. Recently, and nearly overnight, Nokia snatched 20 percent of the world's cellular phone market. Because of examples such as this one, managers have adjusted their view of just how acute competition can be. Defensive strategy must be entirely retooled to address potential competition that comes from companies or joint ventures in remote parts of the world.

Competition will grow in the human resources department as well. As executives network and extend their global reach, they are making themselves better known to foreign and domestic competitors. Some may even inadvertently be positioning themselves as attractive job candidates. Thus, noteworthy defections should occur in nearly all global industries. And the trend will continue, as a larger portion of the business world is pulled into our backyard by way of better communications and a increased international presence.

Judging by these trends, what will the face of business be in the near future? The model company of the 21st century will be centrally directed by multicultural, or at least cosmopolitan, executives. They will set the tone and strategy of the company while leaving local entrepreneurial managers plenty of room to administrate. By virtue of their diverse backgrounds, such managers will be adept at selling similar products worldwide or offering the same services in dozens of countries (provided there is demand). Their most complicated task will be making sure that company operations blend in locally. As in the case of South Africa's large Soweto market, management will be sought that fits in with, or that is even a part of, the local economy.

Brought on by better communications and a growing awareness of market psychology, the new method of doing business will involve staying close to the action (recall Whirlpool's CEO, who spends half his day in global link-ups with district managers, listening as well as guiding). The proliferation of regional markets with specific demands will enable businesses to pay increasing attention to what local customers want. As a result, the search for new ideas, tactics, and technologies will have to accelerate and expand for companies to remain viable.

Executives must also encourage the sharing of information and innovation throughout their companies. As always, they must be prepared to reward the work of their subordinates with personal recognition, continuous training, and a good living. U.S. businesses have for the most part learned this particular lesson. However, the common executive practice in the 1980s of looking for managerial secrets by studying and visiting Japanese companies has been supplanted by a newfound, and instructive, introspection. We are looking at the successes of our own, and are rediscovering the merits of teamwork.

Benefits of Multicultural Management

Management by multicultural employees who have visibility within a company, even a direct line to headquarters, is a trend that also arose in the 1980s. While many companies made these changes to promote ethnic equality, most companies had little choice but to follow through with the same efforts as a straight business move. When multinationals were struggling with increasingly important international operations that were stuck in low-gear, they had to start searching for practical solutions. The problem was that foreign offices were largely redundant knock-offs of corporate headquarters, with little attention paid to cultural gaps. Even regional operations were largely uncoordinated. And too often there was such a tug of war between offices of the same company abroad that competition with rival companies suffered. The top executive in one country reported to both a regional boss, and a product-group chief, rather than straight up the line.

In the 1990s, the top executive's culturally savvy counterpart has much more direct access to headquarters, facilitated by a richer flow of information, guidance, and a better understanding of what works best overseas. Although companies were forced to take the high road—the hiring of multicultural managers—not by mandate, but by necessity, the profound lesson learned is that the move was ultimately good not only for company goodwill, but for the future of business itself. Natural market forces found harmony with social good. When business proceeds smartly, this is often the outcome.

Teamwork has taken on a more developed meaning in today's business world, as employment roles broaden to address new global objectives. District managers are now even encouraged to behave entrepreneurially. It is not uncommon for a foreign executive to spearhead and strike a deal with another global company or to initiate business with "native" companies. Credibility suffers when a foreign manager has to constantly check back with headquarters and seek permission for every step of a deal. Rather, tapping into the manager's expertise is the surest way to cut a path straight into the heart of the marketplace. In addition, managers are in some ways acting as distributors in their own right. If they can push their company's product, that's great. But if they can't, they move to the next level. They engage their company in market research in an effort to better fit their product to local demand.

It's important to remember that it is in the interest of companies to offer up the same product for the same application globally. That is, the widget designed for use in the U.S. should be identical, or very nearly the same as, the widget being manufactured, assembled, or sold overseas. Production standards should be universal, or company and product reputation invariably suffers. Texas Instruments semiconductor group president Thomas Engebus puts it plainly by saying, "We want every product possible to serve the entire world." Not only is this a great way to slash design-and-build costs—it's the ideal. We've seen how demand in localized markets differs. Even the McDonald's menu in China differs from the U.S. menus. But in the model world, universal acceptance of the same product would be the ideal, and is a goal many global-bound companies are striving for.

Managing and capitalizing on information will be crucial to developing the kind of organizations that will thrive in the global marketplace. "The game is shifting from capturing the benefits of scale to developing and diffusing the benefits of information," according to Christopher A. Bartlett, an international-management specialist at Harvard business school. "It was simple when it was all in the home market, but it is much tougher to use the world as a source of intelligence and expertise."

Technology and the Global Business

Acquiring advanced E-mail and other information systems is an important part of the initial process of going global. Teleconferencing and video-conferencing are expected to become more affordable as their usage becomes more widespread. GE Medical Systems alone does more than 1,000 hours of teleconferencing yearly, and other countries are catching on. Small

Foreign-born managers can be helpful in setting up beneficial joint ventures.

and large service companies are developing symbiotic relationships with multinationals, following them around the globe as they set up more and more shops and demand more and more link-ups. Companies are spending liberally on corporate networks too, due to the pervasive fear that local phone systems in developing countries may be inadequate for their needs. Out of sheer frustration with the local system, Cementos Mexicanos, the dynamic cement manufacturer, installed an information system that tracks every part of its multinational empire and that completely circumvents local phone lines. Unilever PC has 31,000 employees using either E-mail or Lotus Notes for communication. The company also uses a Hewlett-Packard program that broadcasts a live tutorial session from its studios in the U.S. and Europe to Unilever employees anywhere in the world. Currently, Unilever has an enterprise-wide satellite training system on the boards.

Joint Ventures, Alliances, and Task Forces

As for gaining market intelligence and prowess, the new breed of execs are aware of the power of alliances and joint ventures. For companies with limited capital, joining forces may be the only way to expand overseas—and that is precisely what's happening. Many have discovered that finding the right partner, regardless of nationality, is the key to global success. And foreign-born managers are instrumental in orchestrating successful partner match-ups. Again, this illustrates the necessity for face-to-face relationships. Though an executive may be entrenched in business back home, the foreign-born manager will be that executive's ears. When Unilever wanted to crack the Chinese ice cream market, it joined forces with

Sumstar, a state-owned Chinese investment company. Together, they formed a venture called Wall's (Beijing) Company. Sumstar's help with the Chinese bureaucracy was critical in getting a high-tech ice cream plant up and running in Beijing in just 11 months. Also useful was Unilever's special task force—a team of Chinese-speaking troubleshooters. In addition to acting as troubleshooters during the start-up of the ice cream factory, they helped to build plants to make other products like detergent, shampoo, and even tea. In America, "speed teams" often do the same work. Texas Instruments employs a comparable "speed team" of about 200 professionals, whose specialty is pushing rapidly into markets. Under the moniker "the Nomads," they have set-up computer chip factories in Italy, Taiwan, Japan, and Singapore. Similar squads from the US West telephone company, based in London, have descended on countries abroad to set up cellular phone systems.

Of course, someone must remain to run things once the squads leave. Those charged with running day-to-day activities are usually executives who have been recruited specifically for overseas assignments. According to global headhunter Richard M. Ferry, the following criteria are endemic within in the qualifications of these executives:

- Their companies have sought them out because of past successful foreign assignments (experience)

- They speak several languages

- They are proficient with technology

- They are capable of the autonomy requred for an assignment abroad

- They realize that providing motivation and guidance are essential parts of the job (leadership)

For the first qualification, experience, companies now prefer local nationals rather than expatriates. Locally hired managers are more cognizant of and sensitive to cultural dos and don'ts, and help to diminish perceptions of a "colonial" company image. Operating profits are also helped by their awareness of subtle changes in consumer habits, customer complaints, and government regulations.

An example of such a new, young executive trainee is Justyna Pisiewicz, recruited by the Boston-based Gillette Co. in Poland (one of the 28 foreign countries where Gillette has offices). Pisiewicz holds a degree from Beijing University, and in addition to speaking Polish and Chinese, is also fluent in English and Russian. Like other Gillette trainees, Pisiewicz first underwent a probationary run at the local operation that recruited her. Then she spent an 18-month apprenticeship stateside with a mentor. Thereafter, she went back to Poland, the norm being to return to the place where originally recruited. After the final rigorous interviews with management, Pisiewicz became a member of the local management team. And as is typical, she will use her extensive training to pursue new business, though with a decidedly entrepreneurial flair.

In terms of giving foreigners clout by offering them key positions, oddly enough, Japanese companies are beginning to trail behind other nations. Their flexibility in hiring Chinese managers, for example, is nowhere near that of U.S. companies. Beyond that, in many Japanese companies, nationals still run all foreign divisions and most key decisions are made from headquarters. This is, perhaps, what the late Secretary Brown meant when he spoke of (as he often did) the American multicultural advantage. The Japanese have fallen behind their Western competitors in China and elsewhere due to their unwillingness to grant authority to foreign executives. Takura Ogata's *The Secret to Success in China* criticizes the Japanese corporate elite for its provincialism. The book also happens to be a best-seller in Japan. The book demonstrates how Western companies hire Chinese managers, give them freedom, and reward them handsomely if they do well. But most Japanese companies are still quite hesitant to hire Chinese at high levels. Not surprisingly, many Chinese prefer to work for Western companies, which offer more entrepreneurial freedom and better pay.

Japan's Sony Corp., however, is on the trail to becoming an international trailblazer within its country. Sony has admitted an American and a European into senior management. Indeed, some observers think Sony could soon become the first Japanese company to be run by a non-Japanese CEO. In any case, Sony executives say they will continue to give non-Japanese executives more responsibility. Consider the company's purchase of Columbia and TriStar motion picture studios. Though so far they are losing money on their software venture, Americans are still running the show. Perhaps if other Japanese companies follow suit and hire foreigners, they will regain their competitive edge.

While rewards are high for companies that can produce the right mixture of variables, the new global economy is hyper-competitive. Ethnically diverse and geographically knowledgable management must have feet in several countries and ample skills as multicultural communicators. Accordingly, more freedom is being given to managers. Because businesses are no long ignoring cultural differences—and in the process, alienating themselves from the marketplace—sales and profits are increasing. At the outset of the global explosion, perhaps few realized that companies could make great strides by increasing their cultural sensitivity.

Chapter 6

Marketing to the World

In the global economy of the 21st century, obtaining marketing information on other companies will be easier and cheaper than what we're used to today. Elaborate marketing plans will become increasingly typical for globally marketed products. But due to recent breakthroughs in related software, the cost of production will not necessarily rise. "Cheap information" will also become a more pertinent factor, as regional development initiatives, U.S.- and state-sponsored trade organizations, and other related agencies will be open sources of facts and figures. Little or no costs will be accrued by those taking advantage of these resources (see the itemized list in the Appendix). Moreover, these groups, often sponsored by the DOC, are beginning to receive more funding.

It is the Clinton Administration's sincere hope that more U.S. businesses will start looking abroad. As mentioned in previous chapters, efforts have been made to see that exporters do not go into markets rudderless. The DOC has been charged with the task of pushing the Administration's programs—even taking in hand the small businesses that it once eschewed in favor of the multinationals. It's anyone's guess, though, as to how long the government will coax businesses off of domestic soil. Some are even now questioning whether the DOC will fold. But the war House Republicans are waging against it is more about bureaucratic bloat than it is about free-market philosophies. Government, partisan or bipartisan, is not interested in pushing isolationism or protectionism on businesses. Rather, it is looking to see that its business and tax bases expand.

Currently, non-U.S. companies can get almost any kind of information they want about U.S. businesses at a nominal cost. Unfortunately, U.S. businesses have been discovering that this is not always a two-way street. However, the quality of information will improve as accounting practices, securities disclosures, and other business-related aspects gain universal standards. And as long as there is relative peace among nations, U.S. businesses will begin to enjoy the same quantity and quality of information overseas that is available here for outside interests.

It's important to note that all of the legislative advances that should facilitate entry into foreign business territory do not mean that the marketplace will become accessible to every business. Utilizing the gains made by the availability of cheap information, and putting the information to work within a global marketing framework, will be expensive. A typical small business will not be able to gain market share for a product or service without a measure of sustained promotion. Look to the global movie marketplace for one example. Hollywood budgets are soaring, and the media would have us believe that it's entirely the fault of skyrocketing checks to stars—$20 million and up for Jim Carrey, Sylvester Stallone, Mel Gibson, Tom Hanks, and others. But the truth is that more is being doled out for pushing the product in the marketplace than for increases in talent salaries. Hollywood

blockbusters are costly to make, but they also carry heavy advertising costs.

And action movies full of expensive special effects and stunts aren't made with just U.S. audiences in mind. Stallone gets his $20 million because audiences love his films abroad, even though they may perform marginally in U.S. theaters. Creating brand-name recognition globally, and often in only a few weeks time, is very expensive. With the competition remaining fierce, studios have found themselves reacting by fanning the flames with even more cash. Like the experience that awaits many small businesses going global, filmmakers are finding that studying a market and deciding which films to make and distribute there is easy and relatively cheap. Acting on the information, however, becomes a wholly different financial matter.

For many companies, the important question to answer in the next few years will not be *whether* to market globally, but *how*. As the world becomes increasingly "virtual," the goal will be to create a climate around products that also addresses and appeals directly to the global consumer. That's why Japanese automakers have given such incredible business to cutting-edge American ad agencies like Chiat/Day. Creative "idea people" are connecting to Americans and their unique sense of culture by featuring dreamy ads, online playgrounds, special offers, "keys," add-ons, contests, and direct-mail promotions. Consider the Japanese automakers' investment in marketing a portent for all global businesses: Locals know the local market.

A prerequisite to implementing an elaborate marketing campaign is to identify the demographics and social issues involved in particular markets. Next comes the challenge of combining novel business methods with an appreciation for a country's distinct social, economic, and political conditions. It's true that to fully identify and uncover all these issues would be costly, but it's an extremely important investment to make in a global marketing program. Recall the example in Chapter 1?—do your homework, then once you're finished, do it again. You may have a difficult road ahead, so you should really know your market. It should come as no surprise, all things being equal, that the selling to and education of distributors and customers may be more difficult and critical to your product's success abroad than at home.

Small businesses going global may also want to look into fashioning their marketing programs after those companies that have seen success with similar products or services in the same marketplace. Small businesses may even be at an advantage. Give your attention to the methods of similar-sized or even mid-sized companies rather than borrowing ideas from the multinationals. These behemoths—big enough to have subsidiaries in several countries—have long been criticized for their insensitivity to other cultures. Although old attitudes seem to be changing for the better, large corporations once discounted the importance of marketing programs—and got trounced for it. Thousands of successful mid-sized businesses were slipping in under their noses and doing a hand-over-fist export business. As discussed in Chapter 5, however, in recent years the multinationals have really begun to get their acts together, but that still doesn't mean that the small business manager should flatter them with imitation. The flexibility small businesses have can boost adaptability (and hence, success) in foreign markets.

The size of the market sought and the approach taken will likely involve different strategies for each separate foreign territory. The lesson here may be that each company's global development will be different and more or less appropriate to each host country. In the meantime, the compelling examples offered by the experiences of other small to mid-sized companies are instructive guides for the search for marketing clues and models.

Selecting an Export Destination

The path of least resistance will naturally be the most inviting entry for entrepreneurs. American companies, for example, can take advantage of NAFTA, the high-profile, low-tariff pact and trading bloc, by selecting markets in Canada or Mexico. Each year, North American tariffs are being lowered in conjunction with NAFTA. Scores of American exporters who have landed contracts north and south of the border are acting on these changes. Consequently, the DOC and other trade groups have been able to collect demographic and other data on behalf of American businesses—helping to alert them of new opportunities and cultural changes.

Canada is perhaps the most appealing candidate for first-time exporters. There is a degree of comfort with its similar business practices and more or less universal use of the English language. On the other hand, while Mexico is viewed as a more difficult market than Canada, it is also considered more dynamic. Its population is three times the size of Canada's, and its percentage of children under 15 years of age is more than double that of the U.S. To be sure, the 86 percent of the *Fortune 500* (MFG) companies that now have operations in Mexico are cognizant of these facts. Increasingly, an upwardly mobile middle-class characterizes Mexico. In fact, middle-class growth is becoming a trend in all of Latin America.

As exporters find that the water isn't that bad, they are beginning to jump in and swim for more distant shores, some going halfway around the world. In 1994, 12 percent of small-business exporters chose Western Europe to do business in. An equal percentage chose the Pacific Rim.

Select your target country by evaluating its friendliness to importers.

Wherever they're going, small businesses should definitely favor countries where arrangements are more or less open to discussion. Remember that duties, quotas, tariffs, and the higher cost of distance delivery will add up to potentially reduced profits. Also keep in mind that no country is identical to another, though several do share similar cultures and markets. The difference in your choice of markets may then come down to choosing a country that is more friendly to imports. Equally important are the kinds of partnerships opted for in particular countries. That is, are manufacturing contracts, licensing agreements, or joint ventures favored? Again, look to the countries that are open to discussion.

Many businesses have found that the process of country selection is really a process of elimination. Marketing research may point to several viable countries (or particular locations within those countries) for your product. But it's unlikely that any small or even mid-sized company is going to implement, or be able to afford, a marketing

and advertising blitzkrieg—which, in turn, necessitates an elimination process. One way to begin is to look for countries against which there is a U.S. embargo on any of its goods or services. The exporter should also consider whether any other of its potential activities abroad are precluded by law. The final step would be to check for potentially unstable political conditions in a market under consideration in order to rule it out.

There are also more conventional considerations. Countries such as Sri Lanka, Paraguay, or Liberia would be questionable markets for businesses selling advanced industrial equipment or scientific instruments. These are products that require elaborate service and support. Backup centers are absolutely necessary, but setting them up in these countries is known to be notoriously difficult. Of course, this information applies only to the fields cited above, but certainly you can draw parallels and conclusions about what sort of secondary attention your product or service may require elsewhere. Look into how and what might result when you make servicing forays into a marketplace that originally perceived you as a product importer only. Good market research should address any worries you have or problems that are imperceptible at the outset of your overseas endeavor. It should also introduce you to potential nightmares you could never have dreamed up.

Cautionary examples abound. If you are a distributor of whiskey or fragrances, reconsider any thoughts you may have about moving your product into Peru, Bolivia, or Bangladesh. These countries levy as much as a 300 percent duty on the landed value of such goods. And public outcry or fundamentalism is not the reason—shortages of hard currency and ever-growing debt are. Determining the strength of a country's economic footing is also wise. Your search may have been diligent and possibly even turned up a lucrative market, but if there is a threat of mind-boggling tariffs, forget it. You might find yourself pushing more money into government coffers than you would have otherwise spent on name recognition in a more open, albeit more competitive, market.

As another example, a business considering exporting a soft drink to India will discover a government that also levies high tariffs in order to zealously guard its local markets. An alternative would be for the firm to undertake a joint venture with a local bottler. But this raises a new set of questions: Should it be a majority or minority venture? Is the rupee convertible? If so, can profits be repatriated? And these questions haven't even taken into consideration the vastness of the Indian market and the difficulty of communications and transportations there. For the exporter committed to entering this market, there are solutions short of giving up on India in favor of a developed country. The business could deal with a local Indian bottler with its own network or means of subdistribution. Or it could become the master of its own fate by distributing the goods itself. These critical choices should be made after conducting a formal marketing survey. As in the whiskey and fragrance example above, the soft-drink maker's survey might indicate an unquenchable thirst for its product, but if the cost of getting it there is too high, the endeavor makes no sense. It's akin to finding an enormous vein of gold, but only being able to admire it because mining and extraction costs are too high to justify.

There are scores of other concerns that also must be addressed in choosing a country and then finding a partner. Is your product a perishable food or medicine? If so, the target countries had better have at least one distributor who is fully equipped to adequately store and refrigerate them. And what if there is just one distributor capable of doing so? The answer is passion. You will need to find a distributor who is passionate about and willing to put in the additional legwork or you may find it spurned and growing old on the shelves.

Perhaps you wish to market in Switzerland. The survey should tell you that the country is trilingual (German, French, Italian) and that the market, therefore, is probably segmented accordingly. On secondary queries, you will see, if your product is electronic, that it will have to work on 220v/60hz, whereas the stateside standard is 110v/50hz. The next consideration will be in regard to the distributor. Is it ready, willing and able to promote the product in three languages? Or could it be possible that you might find a distributor that is also pushing voltage adapters and could sweeten your deal? Example after example in this book has deferred to the importance of finding a good distributor, but the point is essential. If you are able to find one that is willing to sell your product in three languages, you are onto something good. Should the distributor price it accordingly for the market, you are

Finding a partnership that works is key to your success.

onto something even better. And should it help you lower marketing costs, possibly by one of the cheapest yet most effective means available—word of mouth—you are onto something great.

Other considerations in the race toward expansion might take a business to Nigeria—Africa's largest market. But if an exporter's product requires a high literacy rate, it might need to reconsider. Nigeria's might be deemed too low, regardless of entry conditions. Argentina's cosmopolitan market might seem attractive, and studies could indicate a demand for the exporter's product, but because the country favors protectionism, the favorable conditions may be a moot point. Other questions abound, and some of the answers only come through actual experience, regardless of initial research. Do you go through the time and expense

of registering your trademarks and brand names in a small but promising market like Chile? Or do you roll the dice and hope nobody will steal them? Or, possibly, do you watch your product's performance and wait for the market to tell you what to do? If your business is in consumer electronics, you'll find that registering them with the appropriate market will be costly. Look into the experience of other businesses, such as TUV in Germany, BSI in the U.K., Demko in Denmark, or Semko in Sweden.

Registration costs must be factored in as part of your aggregate marketing costs. Until you're registered, your product can't be sold, and that puts you squarely in the realm of the revenue-dead start-up phase. Should your product take off and start producing needed revenues, you may find yourself looking into nearby similar markets under different jurisdictions. You can save yourself some trouble, and a bit of money down the line, if you initially seek out trading blocs in which registration in one country is tantamount to registration in all member countries. In any event, look for the answers beforehand as trial and error can be costly.

After hurdling legal barriers and clearing registrations, a business should again focus on its product. Besides such questions as perishability and technical compatibility, a good deal of time should be spent on research and development issues like the choice of brand name and the color(s) and material(s) of the product and packaging. Determining pricing is also part of this process. Perhaps this is why so many exporters view the market survey as their lifeline to global success. The survey covers the economic, social, demographic, geographic, and even political attributes of each country in which a business wishes to sell its goods or services. Later in this chapter, an outline of market survey considerations is provided.

Choosing a Market Surveyor

Determining who will conduct the marketing survey is also very important. The right surveyor can make or break a company just as easily as its choice of a distributor. It's that crucial. A good market survey can be one of the keys to a business's success abroad. While sources that reveal the juiciest markets for goods are plentiful, they often come at far too steep a price. In fact, as more and more businesses look overseas, they will meet all sorts of international trade specialists, who in truth may be little more effective than an industrious MBA student hired for the task.

Should a business wish to pursue the idea of hiring a student to conduct market research, it can contact the international department of any reputable business school, either at the undergraduate or graduate level, though the latter will most likely be much more knowledgeable and the price difference between the two shouldn't be significant. Students working towards a degree in international trade are usually quite happy to write a market survey for a given product in a foreign market. Many times, these surveys are excellent, and are almost always a fraction of the cost of a survey conducted by a market research company. You may very well be getting the work of a student whether or not you explicitly seek it out. In fact, some market research companies hire out students to complete the work before passing it along to you at a premium. While no business expert would advocate that you put the life or your product in the hands of an unskilled practitioner, it's helpful to be aware of your options in the search for the lowest cost entry into global markets. Businesses short on funds would be well-advised to do a great deal of the leg-work on their own in order to keep costs down before bringing in a professional. The Appendix offers some tips to get you off and running. At some point, however, it is important to employ an expert—even if you are only looking for a survey and not an in-depth study.

To supplement your study, you may want to read business and tourist magazines, which provide a wealth of information for global venturers. Foreign embassies and consulates print pamphlets and brochures related to the historical, economic, and cultural make-up of their countries. Though this is all helpful, it is unlikely that a business is going to be so naive as to make a move based on pamphlets and magazine articles. But keep in mind that survey information will come from endless sources and those mentioned may give you headway into the paper trail you are likely to embark upon.

Product Prequalification

To start the survey process, the surveyor can check to see that products or services fall into one or more of the following categories:

☐ The product is preeminent in its domestic market.

☐ The product's landed cost in a foreign market will be lower than that of any major competitor's.

☐ The product can compete qualitatively with similar or identical products.

☐ The product or business offers a utility, instrumentality or labor-saving technology that cannot, as yet, be readily duplicated by either domestic or foreign competitors.

☐ The technology has patent protection in major countries.

☐ The product has a special flavor or cachet that may make it appealing to many buyers (like the American muscle cars on the streets of Tokyo and Rome in the 1950s and '60s).

☐ The exporter occupies a place in its field in which it is strong enough to fend off existing competition, but not so widely popular as to attract the attention of stronger competitors.

Primary Queries

Uncontrollable factors facing a business's entry into a foreign market will equally affect the survey. Areas to be addressed to make you aware of such factors should include the following:

• What main languages are spoken in business and everyday life, and is there a segmentation of markets by dialects or languages? *Recall the example of the distributor in Switzerland, covering a territory that speaks German, French and Italian. Quebec hosts two languages and Russia, though partly disassembled, has more dialects than it does regions. Other considerations include education and literacy rates of the populace (a real concern for software and publishing-related enterprises).*

• What do the geography, history, and topography of a country indicate about its inhabitants? *The surveyor should look for clues in the lay and location of the land and should study its history. Important factors will include whether the country is land-locked and/or mountainous. Average seasonal temperatures should also be studied.*

• What is the current political situation, and what type of government is in place? *These factors, while often nebulous ones, can kill even the most promising markets. The researcher should look into the country's history to determine whether it is a hawk or a dove.* How would the country's government be characterized? *Is is pluralistic (democratic), socialist, fascist, a monarchy, an oligarchy, a dictatorship?* What are its known and recent policies and attitudes towards foreign investment? *Is it biased toward* laissez-faire, *toward heavy protectionism, or somewhere in between? Are markets open, or restricted and heavily protected, or closed for all intents and purposes? What are the attitudes toward America and its products?*

- What is the macroeconomic condition of the country? What percentage of the labor force in a particular country is involved in, respectively, the primary sector (agriculture), the secondary sector (industry), or the tertiary sector (services)? What is the GDP/GNP? What is the income per capita?

- What is the country's monetary policy? What is the history and strength of its currency in relation to that of other foreign markets? How tied to the dollar is it? How stable is the currency? How frequently is it devalued? What are the restrictions on the movement of funds? How convertible is the currency? How easily can funds be repatriated? What are the country's reserves of hard currency and limitations on foreign exchange? What are the major banking institutions and how healthy are they?

- What are the current import regulations? What are the overall tariff policies regarding industries and products? What are the tariff structures regarding raw materials and commodities, semi-finished products, and finished products *(recall the shock the computer supplier received when France billed him*

for value-added tax). Consider too customs brokers and the impact of import duties on landed costs.

- Will the ISO 9000 Certificate be required? *All companies in the EEC and an ever-increasing number of U.S. companies require that their domestic and foreign suppliers be certified to operate their businesses and manufacture their products in accordance with detailed and exacting ISO standards. The certificate requires that all aspects of manufacturing, safety, quality control, and so on be standardized. Trade centers or DOC district offices can tell you how to qualify and bring your business and products in line with the set standards (see the Appendix). Also, most marketing research companies should be able to provide qualification information.*

- What are the tax structures across the board? *Consider a country's income taxes, its corporate and dividend taxes, value-added taxes, sales and excise taxes, personal and property taxes, taxes paid by nationals versus expatriates, and even discretionary taxes (in the Chapter 1 example, as levied by the Thais against Chrysler for its storage of cars there). Look at organization laws, laws regulating local companies versus foreign companies, laws affecting minority and majority joint ventures, laws affecting foreign office branches, and laws that might impede subsidiaries. Make sure that your surveyor also uncovers any possible anti-trust regulations.*

- What are the distinguishing characteristics of the labor market? What are the applicable labor laws regarding vacation, health, insurance, retirement, and pension plans? How available is the supply of skilled and managerial personnel? What are the training expenses? Are labor unions strong and well-organized?

- Has the country adopted and adhered to international patent and trademark conventions? Is local legal counsel available and competent? Will knowledgeable tax professionals be sought? Do consultants exist, and if so, are they out of your price range?

- What is the social and cultural make-up of the country's people, and what are the pertinent social trends within the economy? What races and religions are dominant within the marketplace? How do the customs and traditions among the population define the particular regions? What is the rate of population growth? What are infant mortality rates? Where are the main cities and industrial hubs, and what is their proximity to each other?

- Finally, what are the infrastructure considerations? *Perhaps more than anywhere else, problems here can indicate the potential for heartbreaking struggles. Spend some time assessing the condition of roads, rails, air, and water transportation systems.* How efficiently are people and goods being moved around the country? How often do flooding or adverse weather conditions impair transportation—for example, will that smoldering volcano in southern Mexico wipe out all your preferred or essential routes of travel? How advanced and effective are communications and postal services? How are other companies solving communication problems—are they using local phone services or have they gone to the expense of completely circumventing them? *You should prepare yourself for frustrating delays if phone services are poor and you plan on entering a market on a tight budget.*

Secondary queries

Secondary queries will help evaluate potential buyers, the competition, the optimal distribution system, pricing strategies, and certain pitfalls and obstacles a company may face in doing business in chosen countries. Such queries will be directed at the following areas:

- What is the identity of the marketplace? What are the demographics of your targeted market, and what is its buying power and past behavior toward your type of goods or services? *Unless you are a pioneer, examples should exist.*

- What are the procedures most commonly used to enter that market? Is access best and easiest via imports, exports, local associations (such as joint ventures), or through direct investments by way of contract manufacturing, branch offices, or the creation of subsidiaries?

- What is the size of the overall market collectively, and—in terms of private companies and public institutions—individually?

- What and how many local, foreign, and U.S. manufacturers in a business's industry are already exporting into the targeted country? How successful are they? How much room is there for new business?

- What are the strengths and weaknesses of the competition in terms of brand awareness?

- How are potential competitors pricing and advertising their products in the marketplace?

- What is the availability of warehouses and retail outlets? What are their practices? How are other exporters and local competitors utilizing them?

Consider the country's monetary policies, when evaluating your participation in its economy.

- What is the availability of a trained corps for aftermarket servicing?

- What are your product's mechanical and electrical requirements? Will the country of choice be able to facilitate those needs?

In conclusion, remember the point made earlier on in this chapter: information is cheap, but acting on it is not. Good decisions and success often come by way of good information properly applied. If you're going to commit your company or product to the global marketplace, you need to understand the climate of the country or countries you plan to enter.

Marketing and Distribution

Let's assume that your market survey is complete, and your company has decided to step overseas. Your next real concern—beyond legal and registration-related activities—will be the marketing and distribution of your product. Of course, the market survey should have touched on the above, but remember, the survey is not the sole qualifier of all steps required for successful entry into foreign markets. Strategy now becomes all-important. Below are guidelines to employ once you enter this phase.

There are two different ways to market and trade globally: (1) passive, indirect and (2) active, direct marketing. The latter approach will likely prove most fruitful for you, but both approaches are discussed below.

Passive, Indirect Marketing

This approach normally involves middlemen and is not normally deemed optimal. In fact, it is sometimes regarded as shortsighted and impoverished for global trade over the long-term. On the other hand, it often requires little or no expense and can yield immediate results. Using this method, companies basically relinquish the fate of their products to a third party (albeit, one whose priorities may run parallel to your company's). Such an indirect, hands-off method is generally viewed as a glorified means of peddling products on a foreign market. It does not really qualify as a means of international marketing.

However, different kinds of intermediaries are available to help you, and they can be invaluable. Among them are commission agents, manufacturer's representatives, piggybacks (sometimes called Mother Goose companies) and export management companies (EMCs). These go-betweens are limited in their effectiveness, in that they may give you some entry into international trade but not, as stated previously, into international marketing.

Commission Agents. Commission agents and manufacturer's reps do not buy, do not warehouse, and do not always sell. They function mostly as scouts for potential overseas buyers—acting merely as intermediaries between foreign customers and U.S. manufacturers. The agent pockets its commission if and when a sale is made. That is the extent of its efforts.

Piggyback Companies. Piggyback companies act as "carriers" of products that are not competitive with their own. These third-party products are shipped to the customer with their own—making up an entire "package" that a buyer may find attractive. Inevitably, though, this is a poor means of marketing your product. You will benefit from sales, but there are attendant problems. Since your product is a part within a larger package—a cog within a wheel—it may never reach its full market potential. It is tied too directly to the success, or lack thereof, of the piggyback company's conglomerated product. There is no autonomy. Accordingly, piggybacking is nothing more than a method of selling products. Their philosophy has very little to do with marketing, product positioning, and creating name recognition.

Export Management Companies. Export management companies (EMCs) function as the supplier's or manufacturer's export department (manufacturer's reps are their domestic counterpart). If properly used, they will take on all the functions of an in-house staff, such as appointing foreign distributors for a product, managing a manufacturer's sales and marketing efforts, handling shipping and export documentation, collecting funds from international customers, and so on. They can be compensated on a project-by-project basis or by an arrangement with the manufacturer whereby they purchase merchandise and resell it overseas at a profit. Proponents of EMCs point out that they fulfill a vital role—they contribute to the overall export activities of a nation. Those against point out that if American business owners could commit to active direct marketing, EMCs would be rendered inconsequential. Even some EMC owners have said that they would quickly be out of business if that were the case. Another deterrent is that some EMCs are domestically based, functioning very much like reps with long arms, but no real physical presence overseas.

Some may still opt to go the route of the EMC, as there are advantages. Hiring the services of an EMC requires little, if any, initial capital outlay or risk. American-based manufacturers with negligible international experience also benefit from the fact that they are given the opportunity to sell overseas without most of the usual headaches. Delivering the products to the EMC's front door is all that is required. From there, the company collects payment for its goods. No export expertise or export staff is needed. Even the risk of extending credit is not a factor. So what are the drawbacks? There are none—for the EMC. Clearly, though, it is not preferable over the long-term for the supplier with an eye on a global presence. However convenient the deal may seem, over a few years the rewards derived from it will seem even smaller if one considers the opportunity costs.

Profit is the prime motivation of the average EMC, regardless of the interests of its various customers—the American-based manufacturers, foreign distributors, and overseas importers that it represents. Keep in mind that making a quick profit is what an EMC is particularly interested in. It knows full well that its overseas distribution rights will not last forever. If it does a poor job, it will be terminated, or, worse, your product will be. And if it does a good job, this may prompt you to eventually go direct. In nearly all scenarios, recognize that the EMC knows its life span will be short and is acting accordingly.

If you have the opportunity, someday have a look into an EMC's mailroom. The owner may even show you, with barely concealed pride, the leaflets from a multitude of companies. Look closer and you may find that they are almost all competitors of one another. Ask what will happen if a given product line fails. "No problem" will be the owner's reply, "we'll sell another one." This is hardly the stuff that will make a new exporter successful overseas, but it is perfectly understandable from the EMC's point of view. Not all manufacturers have a choice, though. If money is not available at the onset of exportation, the company may have to use the services of an EMC. But if money is available, a manufacturer using the services of a "go-between" may be displaying a lack of foresight and commitment that may haunt it in the future.

EMCs certainly have a role to play in international trade. But they do not open doors, save for a few happy exceptions, to successful and lasting international endeavors. Handling competitive lines is essential to an EMC's survival. Should its salespeople travel overseas (not all do), the representatives had better have a "portfolio" of competing lines when calling on foreign distributors. If they can't sell product line A, the reps can offer product line B or C to satisfy their customer. Unfortunately, your product line, D, may only be a means to meet the payroll on Friday or, worse, it might just be padding to make it look as though the EMC really did its homework. Ultimately, your company could end up losing in this very important deal. It's all further proof that building market share should be your overriding objective for the future.

Long-term profits hinge on the continuous expansion of a satisfied customer base. It is the cultivation of long-term customers that will bring prosperity to your company. And in international trade, how can you have satisfied customers if your business doesn't establish a relationship with its clientele? Experience proves that if a company can finance a small but competent export staff, there will be greater rewards in the long run. Assuming that a company offers a reasonably good product or service, its new export department will soon break even by distributing and marketing actively on several foreign fronts. Needless to say, by that time the department will be providing decent profits which can be partially reinvested in the worldwide trading operation.

The lesson here is that there is a hazard associated with passive, indirect marketing. The company that first helps you enter foreign markets can only take you to a certain level. Therefore, the only way to achieve your paramount goals is to eventually bypass intermediaries and work directly with overseas distributors. At what point do you make the break? An argument can be made that you could open your own export division if and when your EMC has shown consistent success at meeting sales targets. By monitoring your EMC's activities, you might get a better idea when this break will occur. But even your success up to this point begs the question: Do you know what you sell? Sure you do. But do you know where? If you are still entirely dependent on your EMC, the channel of distribution is theirs, not yours. Consequently, you do not really control the product's pricing, promotion, or distribution.

If and when you do go direct, you may quickly learn that the EMC's marketing methods and channels of distribution were not the ones you would have selected, or would now select, had you utilized active, direct marketing from the beginning. The market's process of judgment may be skewed with an EMC in control—and not necessarily even to the EMC's advantage. You can be sure that your products were positioned by the EMC through foreign distributors for purposes decidedly different than what would have been your own. Go direct if you or the top management of your company is truly committed to the international market. But you must be committed. In the long run it will be cheaper and may save you crucial time in getting a jump on market share. Stay with an idiom that works: If you want something done right, do it yourself.

Active, Direct Marketing

The active, direct approach requires certain expenditures, an export staff, great patience and sacrifice. And it is worth it. There are tangible and rewarding long-term results.

First and foremost, you actively control the pricing, marketing and sales of your products through your own network of exclusive distributors. Thus, you control your own destiny in establishing and maintaining the visibility of your product line. The adjuncts of an active, direct operation may consist of manufacturers reps, trading companies, foreign distributors, or some combination thereof. But, clearly, the most widely used

A qualified export staff will help you achieve your long-term results.

method of entering a foreign market is through the use of foreign distributors. Once a product line has been established in a foreign market of some importance, a U.S. manufacturer may then see the need to go fully direct. This can be done via joint ventures, branch offices, subsidiaries, licensing agreements, or through contract manufacturing. All are touched on below.

Joint Ventures. The joint venture that bridges oceans is not unlike one that would be structured domestically. A different set of rules and laws will apply, but for the most part the concept remains the same. An infinite number of options will be present and most will be dictated by the needs of the operation. This is a joint venture's positive side—the inherent flexibility it affords two or more entities in coming to terms. Conversely, though, a joint venture is rarely a marriage made in heaven since it pools resources from two partners who may ultimately have divergent goals and interests. Ironically, what makes it so attractive—the merging of each partner's interests—is also what makes it so divisive. Nevertheless, joint ventures remain the best method of initial, direct entry into a foreign marketplace as they are done with the help of a local partner. This is particularly true in certain highly protectionist markets whose potential—in terms of size, population, and/or resources—warrants a concerted long-term effort. But this too carries an element of risk. The partner may become the U.S. company's fiercest rival once the association ends. This potential situation brings to mind the harbored fear of U.S. companies clamoring to get into China's huge markets. Once American executives have divulged their secrets, what's to keep them from being shown the door they once wanted to kick down? With U.S. trade secrets in hand, the Chinese could very well capture the local business, and possibly even turn into global competitors besides.

Branch Offices. A branch office merely designates a legal entity, usually a sales office, staffed by expatriates or local employees of the U.S. company. This is the first step a company can take towards gaining a true foothold in a foreign country. At this stage, it is likely that the company is beginning to market and distribute its products internally, even though it may still be working with distributors.

Subsidiaries. A subsidiary is wholly owned by the U.S. company and is normally incorporated in the foreign country—even having its own board of directors, some of whom may be natives of the hosting country. The subsidiary will keep its books in the local foreign currency and will employ local nationals. It will have full control over the main functions of production, finance, marketing, and human resources.

Licensing Agreements. A licensing agreement is an extremely low-cost method of entry into a foreign market. It is sometimes also the last alternative. A U.S. company may have no choice but to license its products in countries heavily protected by strong tariff duties. Or it may be the only option in a country whose geographic location and infrastructure demand high freight charges. Keep in mind that a licensing agreement implies the transfer of technology, knowledge, special ingredients, and/or intellectual property. This agreement requires the U.S. manufacturer to regularly introduce new products—otherwise it may discover that it has spawned a fierce competitor. Once the licensing agreement is terminated—as with a joint venture partner—the licensee is free to pursue business as it sees fit. Innovation, then, may be the licensor's only edge in retaining steady business growth.

The licensing agreement should include key stipulations as to: the scope of exclusivity of distribution (worldwide or local); the level of royalties and fees (the greater the scope of exclusivity, the higher the fees); the frequency of royalty payments; the termination conditions and provisions; the safeguards against or penalties for infringement of intellectual property; any provisions for quality control and reports; the control of sales (units sold and reported); the penalties for poor performance by the licensee; the penalties for lack of servicing and field support by the licensor; a demand for fair accounting methods; the disposition of patents and trademarks; and the division of marketing responsibilities, including public relations and advertising. Under such an agreement, the exporter's return on investment will amount to the royalty paid to it by the licensee on the products sold.

Contract Manufacturing. Contract manufacturing is a variation of a licensing agreement whereby a local foreign company manufactures a product according to the specs and quality guidelines of the U.S. manufacturer. The main advantage for the U.S. marketer is that the arrangement puts manufacturing capacity close to customers at little expense. In addition, the U.S. maker keeps domestic capacity free for other purposes. The pitfall is that there will be a technology transfer. As in the case of the licensing agreement joint ventures companies should be aware of potential dangers. An oft-stated warning implores that you obtain a good lawyer, a good banker, and a good auditor before you even start setting up shop abroad.

Thinking through the planning and implementation of a marketing system is one of the most crucial steps any business will make—especially a business planning a future abroad. Armed with knowledge, you'll be better equipped to sort through the myriad choices on how to go about marketing and distributing your product, and better positioned for global success.

Chapter 7

The Internet: Around the World in 80 Seconds

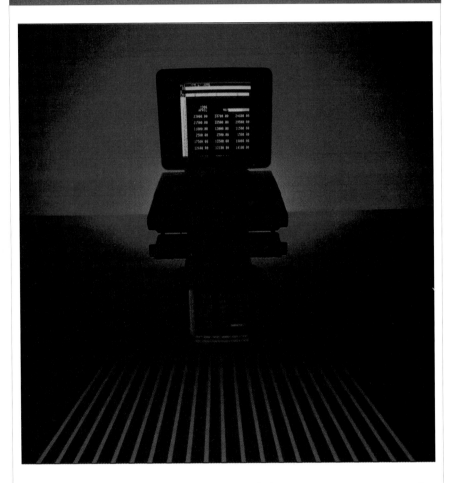

"The Internet is nothing but good news for software... It means the PC is a more relevant device to a broader set of people."

—Bill Gates

By now, we are all familiar with the vision of our future in cyberspace. From Al Gore and Newt Gingrich to Bill Gates and John Malone, academics, business leaders, scientists, and politicians have painted a detailed picture of the coming digital millennium. Already, millions of people who collaborate across computer networks, log on to commercial online services, or prowl the vast Internet are seeing a glimmer of how the vision will come to life. Virtually every conceivable form of information—from stock reports to trade figures to digitized, interactive movies—is going to be instantly available at our fingertips.

A presence on the Internet is absolutely crucial to the small business going global. Plugging into the World Wide Web is becoming tantamount to opening an additional store or another foreign division. It gives the small

Internet accessibility has grown, and so has the number of people using it.

business instant access to information that before was likely not even cataloged, let alone available. How many phone calls and questions would it take to find a distributor for New York wines in, for example, Hungary? Several. But by browsing the Web, the user may have pertinent information within minutes. In 1993, there were only 5,000 Web sites. Since then, more than 300,000 have been created, 45,000 of which belong to business, and the numbers continue to multiply rapidly. Not bad for a technology that's less than a decade old.

As the applications of Internet technology grow, so too do the number of people who have adapted to and grasped its potential. Dr. Ingrid E. Akerblom's research at Incyte Pharmaceuticals, Inc., could be crucial to developing a new generation of superior medicines. But instead of conducting lab work, biologist Akerblom sits at a computer all day, analyzing genetic information that will be part of a giant database program linked to information sources around the globe. With a few mouse clicks, she can zip from her Palo Alto, California, headquarters to Switzerland, Washington, D.C., or St. Louis, Missouri, amassing clues about disease pathology, for example. Just a few years ago, before the widespread use of the Internet, this information would have taken months to harvest from traditional biology experiments, and days to cross check in a library. For Akerblom and thousands like her, the Internet promises new frontiers for scientific research.

Ex CEO of Sunbeam-Oster Co., Paul B. Kazarian, was once trounced by leveraged buyout giant Kohlberg Kravis Roberts & Co. in a grueling battle to buy Borden, Inc. But Kazarian didn't take very well to losing and is now plotting his next takeover by a rather novel approach—the Internet.

His plan could well be cyberspace's first takeover battle. A site on the Web will serve as his command central and bunker.

Kazarian's objective is control of a $1 billion high-tech company that remains unnamed, but when the battle begins, he plans to E-mail shareholders, board members, employees, institutional investors, and the press—broadsiding them with a rush of information that he hopes will sway them to his side. The Internet is an "awesome" tool, Kazarian says. "It's democracy, freedom of speech, and the power to advocate a point of view." However, Kazarian's plans for using the Net may open up a flurry of potential legal problems. Even in the high-tech arena of cyberspace, old fashioned SEC rules apply. One such rule that could impede Kazarian's objective is that it is illegal for holders of 5 percent or more of a company's shares to communicate with shareholders in advance of a takeover attempt. Going online to investors could violate that and other rules. (You can observe Kazarian's process by logging on to his Web site: http://www.japonica.com).

Recall the example of shareholder activism in Chapter 2. It now appears that the Web is about to make the waging of proxy battles even easier. Lens, Inc., a Washington shareholders rights group, recently launched a Web site to distribute research on corporate governance and, eventually, to wage war. "It's the perfect tool, because any exercise of power requires the control of information," says Nell Minow, a Lens principal. Investors going global will do well to look into the approach as more and more privatizations are coming into the marketplace—carrying with them the bellicose old guards willing to fight for their once comfy jobs.

For the exporter, Net promotion should not preempt print, trade show, and other promotional strategies. But doing business on the Web will increasingly become the practice for servicing existing customers and attracting new ones. And although proportionately, there are still many times more Web sites in North America and Europe than elsewhere, a personal computer user can access sites from virtually anywhere. All the user needs is a computer with a modem hooked up to a phone line. But what is the cost? Giant pharmaccuticals, takcover artists, and shareholder activist groups can afford them, but what about pizza parlors, gas stations, and antique shops?

Cost and Equipment Considerations

Currently, the initial outlay for an Internet presence should be about the cost of obtaining a new fully-featured office photocopier. Some say even that is too high. Most of the millions roaming the Web are doing it at work, and not at home, because of the cost. Add to that the $2,000 or so for a multimedia PC, and the know-how to use it, and suddenly there is a barrier to market entry. Taking note are executives at Oracle Corp. and Sun Microsystems. For about $500, they're both offering a kind of bare-bones "Internet appliance" that is being designed just for cruising the Net. "Internet Lite," as such technology is called, will plug right into your TV. If your business doesn't already have a PC, and you're searching for the lowest possible cost of entry, look into it.

Once your business has the appropriate equipment and hook-ups, a site should be able to receive, log, and respond to E-mail. It should also be integrated, if applicable, with other company computing systems. In general, the more flexibility your site has, the better. And the more varied the site's functions and information, the greater the type and number of transactions you can conduct. The result will be that more people worldwide— on and off the Net—will know about the goods and services your company has to offer.

As the information age develops, it's becoming clear that most businesses should take their cue from the Web's existing distributors of soft products (software, entertainment, publications, etc.). It may soon not be sufficient to just sell your products. Rather, a business should aim to offer "keys" that unlock their full potential. Keys are described in more detail below, but basically they are a means for others to find you in cyberspace. A well thought-out key will get customers to your site quicker, making more sales possible. Again, look to others with experience. Regardless of whether you get tips from a direct competitor or a remote player, the information will help you navigate your way through the global marketplace.

An instructive example of a company that has successfully entered the internet arena and maintains an effective Web site is Stream International, Inc. The company handles thousands of copies of software from major manufacturers like Microsoft and Netscape. By the end of 1996, its business of distributing software and technical support to corporations was conducted entirely over the Internet. Under license, Stream had typically cranked out programs on diskettes and CD-ROMs. Then it printed manuals and shipped the boxes of software to resellers. Now it has dumped "the box business," as the company is no longer interested in physically moving their products into retail stores. Stream has found new areas for software-related business—now that it is wholly on the Net, it is moving with ease into a variety of post-sale and direct-to-consumer services. One of these services is a Net-based tech support group farmed out to it by Microsoft. Another is a comprehensive tracking service for the software biggies, capitalizing on its role as an electronic middleman. Stream performs the important task of telling Microsoft and others who owns what and where.

As the experience of Stream and other companies shows, commerce on the Net is burgeoning as well. Even modestly skilled computer users now commonly check the Web for things like a proper zip code, local real estate listings, a second look at an article from a few months back in a local newspaper, Chamber of Commerce events, and endless other possibilities. The Web has become a vast yellow pages of cyberspace whose content is not limited to business.

Users are dividing their attention between noncommercial sites and commercial ones. For business, that's actually good. The noncommercial sites legitimize the Net as a medium, in the same way that a major magazine's editorial legitimizes it for advertisers. The business success of the Web is not all about sales and advertising space. If all the Net provided was names and call numbers, it would be dismissed as merely another Yellow Pages or some other type of advertising circus. The Internet is a social vehicle as much as it is a business or research tool. Partly because of this, it remains a wonderful way to catch customers who are, through demographics and common interests, already pointed toward your product or service. And the benefit is that the added exposure the Net provides comes at a relatively low cost.

For the small business seeking to go online for the first time that finds itself tangled in the intricacies of the Web, or for those wishing to enhance their online visibility, following are a few ways to achieve quicker results.

Achieving Results on the Internet

Within the business, assign a principal or staff member as the designated computer user. He or she should then sign up for relevant newsgroups or online chat groups. The reason is that the user

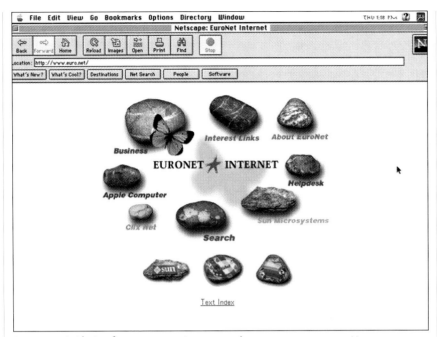

Designing a Web site of your own can give you an advantage over your competition.

can announce the new Web site or changes to the old one. Your company could follow up by placing an ad in an electronic mall full of related products. Gauge the response. If it's satisfying, move on. But if you desire more attention, you can also place listings in an online yellow pages or directory.

The next step is to design a site of your own. Many small-business owners who did not create their own Web sites, but chose a more passive online presence, are beginning to regret having done little more than rent space on a list. Find and engage a Web page designer. Ideally he or she will be local, will understand your area of interest, and will have references (look for more than just the sites he or she claims to have designed and directs you to). Proximity to the designer invariably will make it easier for you to come up with tailor-made visuals and copy for your business. Have the designer use the simplest "keywords" in the home page text so that computerized search engines like Yahoo!, Web Crawler, Alta Vista, or Lycos will take users directly to your page. If you're new at this, it may seem confusing, so

let's backtrack for a moment to what Web searches entail.

Searching the Web

Looking for information on the Web is a little like browsing in a library, where the card catalog is your guide. The Web guides are called search tools, and there are two varieties. The first is Directories, such as Yahoo!, that list Web sites classified by topic. The second is Indexes, such as Lycos, Webcrawler, and Infoseek, that provide a pathway along which specific documents can be found through "keyword" searches. By directing your site designer to use the simplest keys or keywords possible, you make it more likely that your site will be found.

A user may do one of two things: call up a directory such as Yahoo! to search out a general subject and then "drill down" through the material as the search is refined; or he or she may take a more direct route by using keywords. A buyer may have something specific in mind, possibly goods and services similar to yours. In this case, he or she will probably get to your information faster by using the second approach, an index tool. As stated, indexes look through the content of Web documents, as well as their titles, as they sniff-out keywords.

With all the Web navigators out there, there have been complaints that not all navigators lead the browser to the same sites when searches are conducted repeatedly. To be sure your site is called up again and again, keep it simple, and design it to attract the most browsers. A good designer should be able to give you tips on making an attractive and accessible site.

Internet Success Stories

Once you have an initial version of the site operating, your work truly begins. A peculiarity of the Internet is the fact that a small business can have a presence vastly disproportionate to its physical size. A good example of this phenomenon is Hot Hot Hot, a Los Angeles-area specialty hot-sauce store. The Web site of Monica and Perry Lopez's tiny 300-square-foot shop in Pasadena receives as many as 1,500 hits a day from online users. And with all the hits come scores of orders from hot-sauce afficionados across the U.S., Canada, England, Japan, Mexico, and elsewhere. Not every hit brings with it a world of wealth, but the experience of the Lopezes so far has them relieved that they hitched their business to the Internet bandwagon. In the process, they created a heavy demand outside of their own market area, protecting themselves form natural and seasonal fluctuations.

The Web has increased Hot Hot Hot's annual sales by more than 25 percent, to about $50,000. While the result is a far cry from the millions touted by Internet promoters, the Lopezes say that, "when we started the business, we had planned to open a second shop in our second year. The Web became our second shop." The Lopez's ascent into the virtual universe also triggered some business brainstorming. Early inquiries made them realize that it made sense to offer brands of salsa other than just their own. Thus, they are acting as an EMC, promoting whatever the consumer finds most palatable, and crossing brand lines to do it.

Hot Hot Hot is routinely invited to tell its story to business conferences both in the U.S. and abroad. The Lopezes' experience, while positive overall, is not without its ups and downs. Operating a site is a labor-intensive, time-consuming process. One recent challenge was writing more than 400 descriptions for the various sauces they handle worldwide. Additionally, their business requires that they change the content of these descriptions at least once a month. And two hours a day are spent answering the E-mail the site generates. This time commitment, however, is almost certainly less than that of opening a second store, not to mention less costly. Going online keeps the team in the kitchen—where the profits are made.

Hot Hot Hot's success was based on not just a keen sense of timing, but on prudence. The Lopezes gave thought to going online even before opening the store in 1993. Both lacked computer and design skills, so they hired a graphics designer and Web developer in their area. Presence Information Design, of Pasadena, California, did the work and had the site (http://www.hothothot.com) up and operating by September, 1994. The total cost was $5,000, common for a small business. (This does not include the cost of a computer or Internet appliance and applicable software). To relieve themselves of maintaining the site, the Lopezes used Presence Information Design's computers, paying them about 10 percent of the sales generated, an arrangement small business owners on tight budgets should note.

Increased sales from Web purchases can make it difficult to keep the warehouses stocked.

What does the Hot Hot Hot site look like? It carefully mimics the style and decor of their little shop in Pasadena, where rows of bottled sauces sit on pastel colored shelves amid Mexican paper cut-outs and piñatas. Their site straightforwardly reflects the vibrancy, color, and variety of their products—versus the slick textures that are the routine choices of techies and programmers. The Lopezes also used cartoons in an attempt to convey personality and warmth. And to denote important ordering information, comical flaming heads designate the piquancy levels of their bottled hot sauces.

The lessons learned on the Lopezes' journey into cyberspace should work as well with other exporters. You may not field 1,500 hits a day, unless you can come up with an eye-grabbing logo like Hot Hot Hot—but once you've attracted browsers to your site, draw them in with graphics that reflect your product, and that will hold a potential customer's interest. Obviously, you wouldn't choose an element like flaming heads, for, say, medical equipment

sales. But do choose something that goes right to the heart of your product while keeping the potential buyer on the line.

You should think your needs through before calling a Web developer, according to Jeanine Parker, past president of the International Interactive Communications Society and owner of Magnitude Associates, an Internet consulting business in Santa Monica, California. She also advises prospective Web users to consider the cost of starting their own sites, and the amount of money it will take to update it regularly. Beyond that, the substantial challenges of creating a Web site include the time and labor involved in answering E-mail and handling large or numerous small orders. Any Web site competes for attention not only with the hundreds in its class or specialty, but with the tens of thousands of sites across the Web. In either case, the competitors can be sophisticated, multimillion dollar productions. What has helped Hot Hot Hot's site stand out from the crowd, says Parker, has been a very low-tech but highly valuable business commodity: word-of-mouth.

Small businesses going online also must consider whether their products will appeal to Internet users. Hot Hot Hot's customer profile closely matched that of the typical Internet user—most hot-sauce aficionados are men, as are most current Internet users. Once product appeal is determined, says Parker, small businesses must then consider how they will deliver their products worldwide. For example, an order from England took the Lopezes by surprise. As the Web customer punched in his location, the Web computer (server) automatically applied the domestic U.S. postal shipping rate of $4.50—half the $9 cost of shipping internationally. So Hot Hot Hot went manual, fixed the problem, checked into any pertinent restrictions, and sent off a shipment of salsa. In turn, the highly satisfied customer sent in a huge second order. That's when Hot Hot Hot truly recognized itself as an international business.

As they realized their Web endeavor had quickly taken on global reach, the Lopezes realized they would have to program their site's computer (at the designer's workplace) to figure global shipping prices. They saw too that they would have to become Web browsers themselves in order to search out the applicable restrictions and procedures for shipping to foreign countries. Apparently, the revenues they anticipate will more than justify the costs they've incurred to begin their "hot" export business.

Black Bird Pies in Los Angeles is another example of a small business utilizing the power of the Internet. Owner Raven Rutherford had for several years used a van to deliver her homemade pies to individual customers and stores. In 1995, she elected to expand via a Web site. Everything went fine until success hit with a vengeance. A large order came in from Maine, and Rutherford realized she was unprepared to ship the baked goods. She discov-

ered, belatedly, that to do that, she'd need $2,000 worth of special shrink-wrapping equipment and heavy-duty cardboard boxes. Rutherford found herself in the same dilemma as the Lopezes. Demand via the Net had added a whole new side business in addition to her retail outlet. For Rutherford, baking the pies now shares the spotlight with shipping them and negotiating contracts. A site also requires her to spend precious time writing copy and answering mail, and it's likely that she'll soon have to hire someone to help out. Coping with an initial surge in growth may be overwhelming, but the end result—increased business—makes the adjustments worthwhile. A Web site saved the Lopezes from opening a second branch of Hot Hot Hot, and it will likely do the same for Rutherford's Black Bird Pies.

Insurance broker Justin Coates of South Pasadena, California, claims he increased the monthly sales of his firm, Arroyo Insurance Services, from $50,000 to $80,000 by getting on the Net. There are insurance companies that have spent tens of thousands of dollars on their Web sites only to have disappointing results, cautions Coates. But his bargain $1,000 site, with no color or graphics, has succeeded, he says, because he's given it constant daily attention, and provided a high level of customer service to those who log on. "You have to come in, sign on, and download your mail. If you don't make a commitment to do that, you'll fall down," he says.

Net advertisers received heartwarming news recently from a survey conducted by the New York City firm NetSmart. It tabulated the responses of 500 adults who use the Internet and online services for more than one hour per week, not counting time spent on E-mail. Of those surveyed, 97 percent said becoming an educated consumer via their computer is a primary goal. Eighty-one percent of respondents use the Net to research products and services. Forty-six percent of Internet and online service customers use it to buy goods, as a retail device. And 37 percent are online. Few respondents were motivated by leisure-time fun and games. Only 57 percent (for fun) and 22 percent (for games) listed either as primary Net interests.

Cash Transactions on the Net

New-age cyber-capitalists are so convinced of the Net's marketing potential that they've even devised "cyber-cash"—a means of enabling direct cash transactions over the Net. Such secure transactions technology—most of which rely on encryption—are still in test phases, and thereafter must meet government approval. But when they do become widespread, the Net will really take off as a business and marketing medium. Of course, there are detractors who point out the associated risks and the fact that the technology in place is inadequate to secure cash transactions. While scientific researchers are up and running globally, businesses, particularly business transactions, are utilizing the Internet much more tentatively. According to RSA Data Security Inc., safe business on the Net is an idea that's time has come. Using "public-key encryption"—regarded as the best security there is—RSA is luring in big name clients like Microsoft, Motorola, and Lotus. And outside of spy agencies, many think RSA has cornered the competition.

Internet Security Issues

"Public-key cryptography is a cornerstone of the Information Superhighway," affirms Nathan P. Myhrvoid, Microsoft's senior vice-president for advanced technology. "And RSA is the most widely-accepted public-key system." Acceptance didn't come overnight. The privately held Redwood City, California company took 12 years to reach its current size of 45 employees and just less than $10 million in annual sales. But with RSA technology being used by computer and online companies and giants such as Visa International and MasterCard International, Inc., the company is poised to take off. How big? "It'll be a nuclear explosion, " says RSA President Jim Bidzos. He figures revenues will double each year, as long as no one cracks RSA's code. Bidzos is doing everything he can to get them to try: Despite an annual company-sponsored hackers contest, nobody has succeeded.

Public-key cryptography was invented way back in 1977 by Stanford University Researchers. It subsequently became a usable system when three MIT professors began toying with it. They nailed down crucial patents and went on to found RSA. The concept used is that each party in a transaction holds two software "keys." Public keys are published, while private keys are known only to their holders. Both keys are needed to encode and decode a message. For example, to buy flowers on the Internet, you would encode your credit card number using the public key of the card issuer. To complete the transaction, and unscramble the data, you would use your private key. Or, should you wish to send sensitive E-mail, you would zap it along after coding it with your private key. The receiver would use your public key to decode it. Since the public key unlocks only messages that were encoded with your private key, the receiver can be sure you're the sender.

Companies offering security may very well see an explosion in growth as the need for this type of technology increases—which it will as more and more business go on-line with their goods and services. Paying for these goods and services over the Net is another matter. For the exporters making online deliveries, receiving online payments seems only fair. But electronic money is still in the test stage, and it remains among the most challenging issues facing programers. The good news is that creating digital equivalents of checking and credit-card accounts and protecting them with encryption (or public-key cryptography) is a task nearly completed, at least for the short term. However, that's only part of the answer—the rest lies in finding a solution for making "micropayments" for services bought and sold over the Internet. Another issue lurking in the background is that when consumers start conducting larger amounts of business across the untamed Internet, they will vastly increase the chances that confidential data about them will be compiled. Those risks exist now, but are expected to increase, and currently it's very difficult to track computer "snoops." "The potential for invasion of privacy becomes severe," says Don Tapscott, director of the Alliance for Converging Technologies, a private research outfit.

The Digital Cash System

One solution is to create the electronic equivalent of cash—digital money that could be loaded onto your hard drive or onto a credit-card-size magnetic card. The main benefit would be the anonymity we currently associate with cash. That's the idea behind a few start-ups coming on-line now that are planning a kind of private currency system, in which banks would participate by issuing electronic currency to on-line customers. Encryption would protect the identity of the user and help to fend off thieves from electronically pickpocketing you. Your digital cash and coins would go right into the merchant's account, or vice versa. What you had in electronic cash would be equal to what was in your designated bank account.

With a digital cash system in place, anyone with a computer and a modem could sell their wares on the Internet. Although the idea sounds great in theory, the Internal Revenue Service is one group that will probably fight the system's widespread implementation. Due to encryption, buyers and sellers would be dealing in untraceable digital money, which obviously creates a high potential for tax evasion. Banks and credit-card issuers aren't too happy with the idea of a digital cash system either, as it could trigger a loss for businesses specializing in other "conventional" types of money transactions.

Despite all the high-speed networks and powerful PCs to take you into cyberspace—especially the uncharted expanse known as the Internet—it is not yet an entirely safe, hospitable, or compelling environment for business and consumers. Some hackers and con artists thrive on the Internet—but the same can be said of our roads and cities, to which we've adjusted and become cautious. No one in their right mind would walk around midtown Manhattan at midnight, waving a fistful of hundreds around. While in the next few years, we should see the implementation of regulations designed to make the Internet a safer place for business transactions, it's unlikely the system will have a foolproof method of security in place, able to thwart the most sophisticated hackers. However, should a business looking to go global find all this worrisome, there are still the tried and true methods of commerce—cash, credit, and the postal system. Nothing is wrong with proceeding cautiously, albeit slowly, in the secondary, payment side of the Web's marketplace. Leave transactions to the mail while you hammer away in cyberspace, building your presence there. Eventually, a more solid policing system will exist on the Net—and most

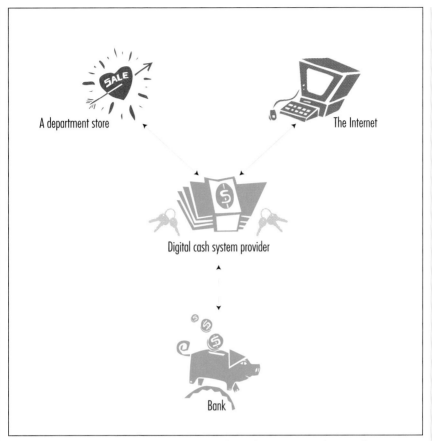

A department store

The Internet

Digital cash system provider

Bank

Digital cash system providers offer a secure clearinghouse for electronic exchanges of money.

computer technologists agree that software developments are the key to creating heightened "virtual" security.

"The solution to everything on the Internet is software," says Edward J. Hogan, senior vice-president at Master-Card International Inc. The players that come up with the programs to protect consumers best, and that help them sort though and make sense out of the vast sea of information on the Web, could wind up at the head of the new world order. "It's like the land rush in Oklahoma," says Lawrence J. Ellison, chairman of Oracle Corp., the second biggest software maker in the market. "The best spot in the valley goes to the one who gets there first."

While the big guys slug it out, there are still plenty of niches for small business. eShop, a four-year-old San Mateo, California, startup, is one good example. The company has come up with three programs to help merchants set up their own distinctive virtual stores. One creates an electronic storefront. Another is a "warehouse" package that manages product and customer information and routes transactions. The third is a browser for electronic catalogs. Although the potential for success seems great, the detractors persist, saying that the business potential of the Internet has been blown out of proportion, for both the big dog and the small-fry.

Capitalizing on a Changing Medium

In the beginning stages of something that seems as promising as the Internet, it may seem that anything is possible. Down the line, we all know what reality can do to dreams. Take the words of author and *BusinessWeek* columnist, Robert Kuttner. "Many prophets of cyberspace think the Internet is the apotheosis of the marketplace. The whole affair is marvelously decentralized and self-executing, with no need for pesky regulations. Any seller can offer wages to any buyer, worldwide. For theorists such as authors George Gilder and John Naisbitt, and for Peter Huber of the Manhattan Institute for Policy Research, the world of computer-mediated communication realizes a market utopia—Adam Smith with a computer. I'm not so sure." Kuttner cautions that the Internet is a product that grew out of a Defense Department program intended to link remote computers to weapons development, research, and other military uses. University and scientific communities picked it up after the military dropped it. Kuttner concludes by asking, "What do the military and universities have in common?

Public money and a severe lack of profit motive."

Early attempts to advertise over the Net were "flamed"—attacked and ridiculed. Internet users enjoyed the free services and information that abounded, and considered ads for paid services or products an intrusion. In fact, casual use and the preponderance of freebies was, and remains, a deeply ingrained ethic on the information superhighway. In its current stage of infancy, the Net is primarily a medium of free information exchange. Understandably, users want the Internet to remain toll-free. With business products and services coming on-line, the Net's once fabled image of anarchy is fast submitting to a well controlled, policed marketplace. Although some veteran users may balk at the changes, newer Internet surfers will come to accept the changing face of the online medium.

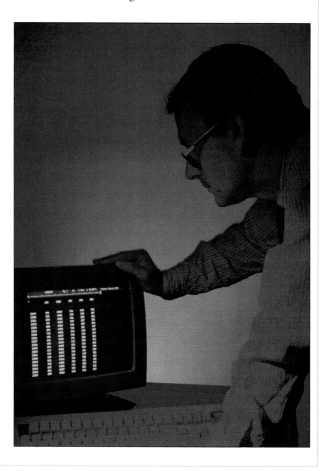

The changing face of the Internet offers a wide realm of possibilities.

Already, many sites on the Net require cash for an exchange of information. And with online shopping about to become more widespread, due to cryptography and other software advances, the nonprofit, casual user is going to be forced to co-exist with businesses seeking profits and customers seeking product. Yet market-watchers are finding it difficult to estimate the extent to which fee-for-service data will drive out free data. That may be determined by the quality and quantity of the goods offered over the Net. Those that believe co-existence is possible could point to our highway system. Truckers share it with salespeople, travelers, joy riders and carpoolers. The only complaints you're likely to hear are if someone's going to fast or too slow.

A last word about security on the Net: Recall the time of the old West, when a town would elect and hire a sheriff who would in turn offer protection to the locals. This sheriff roamed freely, and was largely perceived as the judge and jury as well. On the Internet, with all its wild and woolly ways, communities in the form of companies are setting up their own local gunfighters—by way of software. The programs are being designed to keep the rouges and swindlers out of town, or to catch them if they do slip in. But how soon will it be until the cavalry (in the form of the Feds) come roaring in, imposing a universal standard of laws, regulations, and codes that just over one hundred years ago did in the rugged, individualistic West? The government did create the Internet, so what's to keep them from coming back in? And would governmental regulation of the Internet be good or bad? Your opinion might be formed by your product, and some see government intervention as the only way to provide the order and security their product demands. On the other hand, you might view government entry as a thinly veiled precursor to Web taxation—something nobody wants at this point. The Justice Department continues

to lurk in the background, making sure no one single company takes over the Net's gateways. That's good for competition, but also indicative of an already strong government presence.

For the time being, the Net is a business freeway to overseas markets at an extremely low price. Throughout these chapters, you've seen example after example of the need to go overseas, attend trade shows, visit embassies, lobby foreign government representatives, seek out distributors, and so forth. For the truest form of entrepreneur, the individual with an idea, all this globe-trotting may be just too expensive. Bill Gates, Steven Jobs, and Andrew Carnegie all started with ideas. You can too, and the Net is your fastest way to gain a presence in a market where you may think your product will sell. Consider the cases of Hot Hot Hot and Black Bird Pies. No one was pumping overseas cash into these tiny companies. They are examples of moderately funded entrepreneurs using a little savvy and carrying a superior product. If you offer a quality product that is priced competitively, people will want it. Both those companies are now in the black because of their adherence to such a simple philosophy.

Never underestimate the risk of security breaches, particularly if you are selling services that can easily be grabbed by a hacker. Even if you could follow trails and apprehend the culprit, your reach won't be as powerful in the global marketplace. What are the chances of successfully pressing charges against an Internet thief who resides in Hungary or Finland or South Vietnam? Be cautious right from the onset. Think of how it would feel to suddenly see your work floating freely about the Net, as did writer Douglas Adams. His best-selling book, *Hitchhiker's Guide to the Galaxy*, has been posted there. And guess what his royalties are? Zip.

Finally, add up the cost of going global over the Internet. There's the expense of a wired PC or "Internet appliance," plus the cost of designing and maintaining a site. In the case of Hot Hot Hot, the total cost was about $5,000 plus the 10 percent of sales their designer charges for lending out its computer services. Considering the boon to Hot Hot Hot's business, the initial investment wasn't a big one. And others are getting by much more cheaply. Insurance broker Justin

Coates had a utilitarian, though effective site designed for him for only $1,000. With a $2,000 PC, his total outlay amounted to only $3,000. Of course, there are associated fees, maintenance charges, and phone tolls, but considering the global reach, and the potential, the cost is next to nothing. The Internet is truly is your cheapest entry into a foreign market.

Chapter 8

The Era of Globalized Production

Managers today face a myriad of choices when deciding to go global. With newly opened countries like Vietnam entering the global economy, the small business must seriously consider its global options for manufacturing, outsourcing, and purchasing. New sources of raw materials and other supplies, like labor, are coming on-stream all over the world. And with the impetus of new technology, tapping into the sources will be easier than ever before. This does not imply that the manager's job will become any easier—rather, the opposite may be true. Global decision-making will be crucial to the overseas success of a company.

Decisions were important in the domestic market, but entering a foreign arena increases the scope of managerial considerations. Going global means that there are choices tied into the stability of foreign government and markets, questions of infrastructure, labor, the availability and quality of raw materials, taxation, arcane legal systems, and so on. Recall our example of Freeport-McMoRan's gold mining

Hiring locally can offer your business highly skilled workers at a lower cost than bringing labor in from the outside.

venture in Indonesia. The company is making money, but that hasn't stopped local tribes from occasionally tossing spears at the miners. However, manufacturers continue to step overseas as they find that even with the uncertainties, enormous potential exists. Just as the multinationals discovered the benefits of hiring locals and allowing them some entrepreneurial freedom, small businesses are entering markets and setting up there under the most mutable conditions.

It comes as no surprise that manufacturing is becoming more flexible in the global economy. U.S. businesses will place plants closer to their target customers, while they move design and other highly skilled services further away.

Why the "global shuffling"? Manufacturing placed in geographical proximity with the consumer will not be burdened by high transportation costs. Additionally, businesses can factor in the benefit of a lower cost, though often highly skilled labor pool—plus the credibility "hiring local" gives to a company or joint venture. Outsourcing

design work halfway around the planet, or for that matter, next door, makes just as much sense. It allows companies to pursue an item of acceptable quality at the lowest possible cost. There's no need to take design work to Silicon Valley or Boston when it can be done just as well, and much cheaper, in Taipei, Beijing, or Bombay. High-tech R&D facilities will be found increasingly in less-developed countries, such as the Texas Instruments facility in Bangalore, India.

Technology is the tie that binds global shuffling. Without the scores of recent breakthroughs, it would have been impossible for the small business to oversee so many far-flung operations. Closer-to-market, time-conscious design and manufacturing will be further enabled by a kaleidoscope of digital innovations. Two basic categories in improvements will lead the way: computer chips and cable. The circuit density of computer chips (their ability to process instructions) is now doubling, on average, once every 18 months. Transmission speeds of new optical fibers will have jumped one hundred-fold by the year 2010. Strands of glass thinner than a human hair will carry wideband business communications at hitherto unknown speeds. As product development expertise and capability spread rapidly around the globe, the unit cost of both chips and cable will drop dramatically—enough to be affordable for most small businesses to utilize the technology. Because product cycles will be measured in months, not years, pirating will be discouraged, while legitimate sales benefit.

The ever-more elegant global electronic Web means that breakthroughs in American or Japanese university labs can yield commodity products quickly and at reasonable costs. That's because the knowledge and software tools used for designing electronic products do not require the infrastructure needed, for example, in the steel or petrochemical industries. The basics of designing a circuit can be taught in a classroom or downloaded by modem. Perhaps more than any other American company, AT&T has the most authoritative vision of this future. Put simply, by the early 21st century, components based on light waves will begin to augment slower electronic parts. The result will spawn videoconferencing, with built-in cross-border language translation, that will be as common as today's word processing programs and spreadsheets. Everything is in place for this next phase of the communications revolution, with no major upgrades in the infrastructure required. But the question remains: will the consumer buy into it? Communications specialists are hedging their bets that they will. "The chief technology issue now is not 'can we do it' but 'is it worth doing?'" says AT&T Bell Labs president John S. Mayo. Ultimately, the direction communications technology takes us comes down to profit motive. Keep in mind that business, not government, is directing (and financing) most of the major research and development in the field.

Ours will be a world in which closer-to-market manufacturing will be paralleled by more computer- and network-mediated remote and online services. And not only product outsourcers will benefit. Large U.S. medical centers will be able to conduct remote diagnosis and treatment of patients that are interned in small rural hospitals or facilities overseas. As another example, extensive "digital reserve desks" will meet the research needs of college students around the country. At work, computer designers and software engineers will have the technology to swap detailed chip designs and scientific simulations in real time. Upon us is the once futuristic notion of linkups—where people in separate rooms, continents away, interact as though they are face to face.

As this technology is deployed, major economic changes will occur for small and large businesses. It will be far easier for a small retailer to maintain customers on four continents. Shippers will be able to closely track global package deliveries utilizing satellite global positioning systems. Entertainment and information will reside in vast oceans of digitized data—downloadable from the Internet. And, of course, the Internet will allow payment by cybercash, the electronic certificates with encrypted signatures touched on in Chapter 7. Without glitches, building the new infrastructure will be the job of business, not government. By instituting governance, Net users may possibly never be hindered by government interference.

Meanwhile, existing electronic industries will mature in several countries. Taiwan has done well by focusing on making PC motherboards. By the mid-1990s, its firms had captured two-thirds of the world market. Now Taiwan is moving into networks and low-end telecommunications (since improving its infrastructure with the motherboard profits). How did Taiwan get its start? Through forced commoditization. U.S. firm Chips and Technologies, in San Jose, California, first created the low-priced chipsets used to make the motherboards. The Taiwanese saw an opportunity with their low-wage cost advantage over American companies, and quickly figured out how to make the chipsets and motherboards more cheaply.

In the coming years, more advanced chips will control everything from cameras and cell phones to auto engines and factory robots. Chips will increasingly replace, or at least direct, functions once handled by mechanical switches, motors, and other moving parts. Because the chips can be made at a very low unit cost, prices for the chips and the products that utilize them will remain low. For example, after two years and $15 million in research and development costs, C-Cube Microsystems of Milpitas, California, produced a $25 compression chip that squeezes audio and video data so tightly that a full-length movie can be stored on a single CD. Other American chip makers feed the hankerings of Japan's video game manufacturers. For instance, LSI Logic Corp. built the chip that runs Sony's Play Station. As seen by the example of the Taiwanese "borrowing" from existing motherboard chipsets, there's not much to stop the commoditization of the new order of chips from occurring. However, global manufacturers may actually benefit as forced commoditization becomes a two-way street in the more balanced world economy.

New age product development and the global outsourcing climate will continue to benefit from ethnic diversity. Taiwan and other Asian countries have realized several gains from an ethnic and intellectual link to Silicon Valley, often called the "Chinese Highway." The largest ethnic minority in the Silicon Valley are the Chinese, thousands of whom are engineers, many with advanced degrees from U.S. universities. Similar flocks of digital designers populate the global landscape: Israelis dominate key areas of encryption technology, used in new American cable and satellite-TV equipment; Indians run several of America's most prestigious research labs. Russian physicists and engineers, uprooted by the collapse of Soviet research institutions, have dispersed (many going to Israel and Eastern Europe), though some have surfaced to license blue-green laser and workstation technology to Korean and American corporate giants.

Successful smaller firms will need to continue to outsource design work to multicultural counterparts. They will also forge alliances with global companies due to the high cost of outside product R&D. These alliances will help shelter a small business during downturns in sales of existing products. And during upturns, alliances will generate cash that will help the individual firms diversify into higher-margin products. Indeed, alliances can even be made with competing companies. Two companies that are locked in a crusade to best each other with their existing, competing products may agree to split the cost of a major investment in a next generation of complementary products.

It's important to note that market turbulence brought on by the digital revolution may overwhelm even the alliances advocated above. With the pace of the information revolution running so fast and furious, smaller firms may not be able to keep themselves from being buffeted by leapfrogging technology. Tomorrow's wonder-product might be the day after's losing proposition. And just how many losers can a small company carry? Not many. That's why alliances, even in a fickle, dynamic marketplace, are the best bet to longevity.

The information revolution's biggest unknown for new computer or electronics businesses is the shape of the next-generation telecommunications infrastructure. Europe, America and Japan are putting billions of dollars into high-speed networks of fiber and

International installations of fiber and coaxial cable will make telephone networks a business boon.

coaxial cable. Estimates show that installed fiber and cable will grow by 22 percent through the end of the century—that's a minimum of 10 million miles installed per year. Cellular and wireless networks are also a magnet for massive investment. In fact, the latter may have a slight edge. Companies racing into developing countries are going the wireless route—bypassing the landline phase of laying fiber and cable. This includes phone and audio, and video and TV. By bouncing TV signals off satellites to small-dish antennas on the ground, major satellite service providers can then distribute programming or other services to millions of customers. Hughes Electronics is doing just that. In the U.S., Hughes and Hubbard Broadcasting, Inc., launched a 150-channel service that just reached its half-millionth customer. Now Hughes is offering person-to-person videoconferencing services over high-speed satellite links.

The conflicting infrastructural alternatives—phone, cable, satellite, and cellular—have boggled providers and corporate users. No one yet knows what ultimate shape the information highway will take. The future is definitely uncertain, and open to even the most fundamental questions and frustrations. Just ask Tele-Communications Inc., which backed off its planned megamerger with Bell Atlantic in 1994. Reasons were several, but certainly the board was spooked by the eerie realization that a fog had settled over their global industry. At the same time, few of the multimedia network trials initiated by US West, TCI, AT&T and Time-Warner are making any real headway.

The effects of the confusion are naturally rippling backward to impede research and development, which has triggered adjustments in the process. The search for the modality that will eventually win out has led to an emphasis on cheaper research methods—methods that promise to democratize what remains of infrastructural development. Compromises may be necessary, as creating telecom infrastructure is one of the most capital-intensive activities of late 20th-century commerce.

Supercomputers and elaborate software have already diminished reliance on expensive biology labs or wind tunnels. R&D has never been more productive, thanks to faster information searches, more true-to-life simulations, and better instrumentation. Vastly more sophisticated software is on the desktops of today's scientists and engineers, and now science itself is going digital. At the same time, desk top computers are on their way to becoming as powerful as modern supercomputers. As geographic, and, to some extent, financial barriers dissolve, relatively sophisticated research and development will be put within the reach of smaller companies and nations. This will only benefit underlings in search of ever more sophisticated product development. Scientists around the world may soon run the same computational models as their counterparts at MIT or Stanford.

Indeed, the digital future, linking brainpower around the globe, calls for a completely new conceptualization of international competition as we now know it. Partners profiting together from two very distinct countries and cultures will find that friendship is a possibility after all. And we can look toward that as fantastically powerful manufacturing and outsourcing opportunities become more and more available. Powerful tools are now in the hands of humanity, on and off the assembly line. And that trend should only escalate as the digital revolution continues into the 21st century.

Chapter 9

A Powerful, Borderless Financial Market

emember the Barings and Sumitomo scandals? In the future, the lessons learned will be applied, but not to the point of scrutinizing the flow of money. The rate of trade will only increase as trillions upon trillions of dollars are exchanged daily around the world.

Despite the miscreancy of some of their ranks, the influence of fund managers and traders will rise markedly vis-a-vis that of central bankers and politicians. Managers and traders will essentially impose their will on a gov-

ernment's ability to tax, spend, borrow, or depreciate debt through inflation. Simply put, the movement of a trader's portfolio will be the strongest barometer of approval, or disapproval, of a government's fiscal policies. Such a movement of capital will become tantamount to a vote.

These operatives can cause a huge next-day hangover for a government making a painful decision to, say, devaluate its currency, to undertake trade sanctions, or to otherwise pursue its ends and uphold its policies. The managers and traders will belong to the commercial sector, and may even be stateless, but to try to preserve the value of their investments, they will inevitably guide, encourage, and discipline government decision-makers.

The traders' excesses or abuses will not prevent the market from becoming a more efficient and catalyzing instrument of growth. Instead, it seems we are on the way to a golden age of investment not seen since the virtually unrestrained capital flows of the late 19th century. Global interest rates have begun to converge (although shrewd investors will capitalize on the residual divergence). In addition, regional currencies will arise, in imitation of the EU's recent quest for a single unit of exchange.

What the Future Holds

Dizzying changes lie ahead. More emerging governments, consumers, and businesses will benefit by the direct participation of the smallest investors in the developed world. The professional bureaucrats at the World Bank and IMF will no longer be the principal intermediaries between the First and Third Worlds. Instead, both large and small investors will buy their own equity interests. They will also do their own bidding as they keep an eye toward returns. Look at the level of investment in the Third World. In 1995, it amounted to nearly $200 billion—90 percent of which was from private investors.

The influx of money, however, will inevitably split developing countries into haves and have-nots. And regardless of your take on it, the cuts will be made according to the criteria of developed nations. A cash stampede has graced Argentina, Brazil, Mexico, Thailand, China, and several other nations. But the stampede was triggered by those in First World environments, particularly stock and bond investors betting on such criteria as: the spread of democra-

cy; sound financial, monetary and legal standards; a managerial middle class; and the transparency of corporate accounting. However, countries that were once Third World stars, like Nigeria and Venezuela, are now being shunned due to political strife and fiscal mismanagement. Foreign investors are running away, making them the have-nots once again.

The monetary trading market will only get bigger as world trade and GDP increase. Savers should be able to move funds around the world at will, and the new regional currencies will make trading and political blocs more efficient. The EU will complete its move toward its single currency early in the next century, creating a standard that will certainly ease the flow of money. Elsewhere, the Americanization of global finance will promote the dollar as the primary monetary standard, eclipsing even the EU's standard. Argentina's and Hong Kong's fast-growing economies have already pegged their monetary system to that of the U.S. dollar. The Russians are abandoning the ruble for it. And throughout Asia, the dollar is the denominator for trade and investment. Among other things, this climate makes it unlikely that the yen, however formidable, will arise as a regional currency.

The globalization of stocks will also continue at the same rate. Investors have already poured nearly $1.5 trillion into companies outside their home markets. While much of that has gone into industrial countries, emerging markets are increasingly the focus of worldwide investor attention. Equity capital flowing from the First to the Third World has increased twentyfold since 1988, even though emerging countries account for only 15 percent of world stock market capitalization. But Michael J. Howell, a Barings Securities Ltd. analyst, estimates that that figure will climb to 44 percent by 2010. With the returns that overseas stocks have yielded fund managers (see Chapter 3), money will continue to be pumped into emerging markets for the next 50 to 100 years.

Trading Around the Globe

What can international traders look forward to in the near future? The logistics of individual money transfers will be simplified. Moving capital will become instantaneous and more secure. Borderless rules will evolve to protect consumers from unscrupulous operators. There is also the likelihood that law enforcement of some sort will emerge to combat laundering. This could slow the speed of transactions, but most will willingly abide by any rules put in place to protect them. A further detriment to speed could be the IRS's intervention, particularly if "cybercash" takes off. As discussed in Chapter 7, the philosophy behind cybercash is user anonymity, and that is something the IRS will undoubtedly want to study.

Nevertheless, it will be possible to move cash from, say, the mutual fund of an American pensioner in Baja, California, Mexico, to an industrialist in Guangdong Province, China, with only a single phone call. Conversely, a middle-class worker in a developing country will have access to the West's array of investment tools via new financial markets there. Combining them with the trend toward global wage equality will allow the worker the opportunity to invest in or start up any number of a legion of smaller businesses in his or her respective countries.

By way of example, and as a perspective on the capitalizing potential of the masses in the five biggest emerging markets—China, India, Indonesia, Brazil, and Pakistan—just $400 per capita saved or accumulated via mutual funds or pensions over ten years would yield $1 trillion available for investment. Perhaps that is why the World Bank and the IMF are warning that

highly volatile trading will become routine. For instance, the once relatively laid-back market for municipal bonds and other forms of government debt has already become a $16 trillion casino that behaves more and more like a stock market. To be sure, governments, alliances of governments, and regional authorities may institute policies to restrain the excesses of new global markets. In actuality, however, the reverse is happening. To some, the very sovereignty of nation-states is in question. As financial borders fall, challenges to traditional-national political forces are sure to follow.

Implications of Political Change

The new realities and technologies of the post-Cold War period have, in a few short years, brought three of the world's most enduring "democratic dynasties": the Liberal Democrats in Japan, the Christian Democrats in Italy, and the Congress (I) Party in India. In a world less defined by the struggle against the ominous specter of the "Evil Empire," and increasingly focused on economic competition, a search for fresh values and faces is underway. "All democracies are in a stage of soul-searching," says Takeshi Kondo, director of the office of political and economic research of Itochu Corp., a major trading firm in Tokyo. "Self-identification is a common problem in Japan, the U.S., and even Europe." Echoing this analysis is the former French ambassador to the EU in Brussels, Jean-Marie Guehenno, author of the *The End of the Nation-State*. "We're in for a long period of inventing new political ideas . . . technology is moving faster than politics," says Guehenno.

Voters worldwide are becoming more hesitant to accept a single foreign policy "package" from established political parties—at least those packages centrally dedicated to merely safeguarding

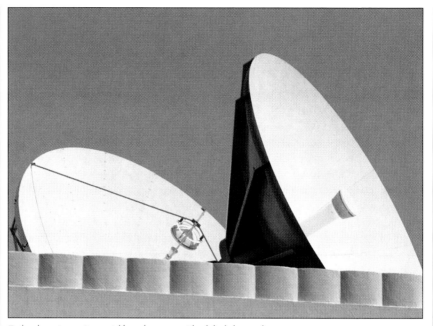

Technology is moving quickly to keep up with global demands.

society from Communism. Today's national politicians are slowly being forced to abandon the vicious cycle of disappointing performances in the face of rising expectations from their constituency. This political uncertainty is affecting politics globally.

In addition to undergoing substantial ferment in Latin America and Europe, constituents are changing the political landscape in the Far East. Japanese voters recently cast blank ballots—so-called "white votes"—in greater numbers than ever. The strong statement signified that no political party answers their needs. In a recent municipal election, the number of white votes exceeded those won by the lead candidate. Even in the U.S., polls indicate a strong public consideration of third-party candidates for the presidency, although such candidates have garnered only a small fraction of the popular vote in the last two presidential elections. Meanwhile, heretofore unthinkable corruption prosecutions have dogged the highest levels of government both in Japan and Italy.

Some see these developments as part of a long overdue housecleaning of the political process. They hope that the fall of the great parties will bring fresh faces, new ideas, and an injection of hope to politically stalemated issues. Others argue that the hope generated by the collapse of the old order will be short-lived. The end result will be increased instability and weak, inexperienced, and ineffectual governments. In India, a huge political vacuum has been left by the decline of the Congress Party—which had governed India for 46 of its 49 independent years. Much like Mexico's PRI, it had become home to nearly all who sought a share of political power.

Now in India, political uncertainty is the order of the day. The first post-Congress government, which took power in mid-May, 1996, lasted all of two weeks. Its successor is a shaky 13-party minority coalition led by a figure with the most provincial of supporters. Congress, the party of mythical leaders like Jawaharlal Nehru, his daughter Indira Gandhi, and her son Rajiv, was once the engine of anti-colonial struggle. Apparently, its charisma and authority have lost the widespread influence it enjoyed over the last half decade. Congress suffered not only from the end of colonialism, but from the end of the Cold War as well.

Possibly, the system suffered most from factionalism and colossal corruption. One-third of the scandalized Cabinet had to resign in the last Congress government, led by Prime Minister P.V. Narasimha Rao. Furthermore, it failed to deliver on its populist promises of a better life for the millions at the lower end of the country's social scale. Perhaps if Congress had taken note of the strong, populous middle class among the Hindus in the north of India, it would have seen that market policies are now at the heart of its country's political issues.

Like Congress in India, the PRI in Mexico has also failed to acknowledge that a more middle-class style of democracy has taken hold in its country. Free-market reforms and the ascension of an aggressive, privately owned, and therefore very independent media, are broadening the wishes and hopes of constituents. No longer fed by the influence the ruling parties held over radio and TV, Mexican voters are holding out for reforms that they feel will directly benefit them. By broadcasting to less developed countries, the new networks of cable, satellite, and digital TV stations, along with scores of private radio channels, are opening up a host of free-speech, political, and cultural issues. In Mexico (and elsewhere), this development has forced the PRI to contend with public opinion as never before. But the new Mexican media has also served to inflame an already heated situation, often propelling conflicts into instant crises with which government decision-makers are ill-prepared to deal.

The Shifting Power Bases

So far, the chief recipients of the power flowing away from once-dominant parties, have been new, regional, or sometimes single-issue parties, and nongovernmental interest groups (such as Greenpeace). But sometimes the power has gone to groups with no direct political connections whatsoever. The best example of this phenomenon is the planned European monetary union (EMU). According to Jean-Marie Guehenno, it's nothing less than an agreement to end the political management of major currencies. It remains uncertain how far the effects of this development will spread across the world, and where it will lead. But it does seem that with the grand threat of communism gone, a more difficult and important question arises: What, if anything, will bind people together politically?

The answer is: the economy. As it was for the American electorate in 1996, so it is for the global democratic electorate of 1997 and beyond. That means that constituents, voters, and special interests will likely array themselves politically according to the best means of benefiting themselves economically. It's no secret that countries will actually compete with one another on capital markets. Equally, constituents recognize that the system will favor and reward those that are best prepared to reform their economies and compete for capital. New and existing parties will create platforms projecting their positive efforts toward facilitating safe and lucrative foreign investment. And political leaders will hold up Southeast Asia and certain Latin American countries as examples.

Some national leaders will still try to defy the market. But that could subject a national economy to steep interest rates or eviscerated equity in privatizations—a situation that could undermine productivity and cause the loss of much-needed jobs. Social tensions could rise, destroying whatever shreds of fiscal stability remain. Those leaders could watch their country's prosperity dry up in a matter of a few years, as occurred in Venezuela and Nigeria. However, a global trend toward human freedom may very well stop any sort of market suicide. Just look at the example of South Africa. Whereas its apartheid policies once spelled embargo, it is now regarded as a global hot spot for investment.

Trends indicate that the great majority of countries will woo, not alienate, almost any source of foreign capital. The increased mobility of capital will force more and more countries to, in effect, "use it or lose it." Just as U.S. locales—with the country's more liberal regulations, looser procedures, and incentives—have lured business, so too will foreign entities. The U.S. government is still relatively indifferent to the increased volume and mobility of capital, but many countries, like Mexico, are more heavily controlled by the fluctuations on Wall Street. Pressure from financial markets will actually cause governments to become more disciplined in their approach to foreign business. The more conservative business atmosphere will mean that governments will still have myriad policy options—but on a case-by-case basis, will be more careful not to blow opportunities for outside investment.

Chapter 10

Security and Techno-Terrorism

Germany   Italy   Norway

on a normal business
European busi-

Security takes on new importance in the global economy. The intelligence services of foreign governments are increasingly spying on business concerns. Companies have always faced security challenges, but in the international arena security efforts are compounded by considerably fewer conventional controls. Businesses must take into account that promoting their product or service ever more widely around the world may subject their company and personnel to economic espionage. Snooping or piracy, or outright robbery could occur.

Worse, terrorism is an increasingly worrisome threat. The fact is, nearly every company in every facet of business—from law firms to construction companies to technology developers to manufacturing operations—faces formidable security challenges.

Corporate espionage can be defined as the transfer of property to those unauthorized to hold it. It entails the removal or disclosure of proprietary materials such as software, formulas, designs, blueprints, strategic plans, personnel files, plant specifications, policies and procedures, and so forth. Piracy is distinctly different as it takes the act of theft one step further. It is defined as the copying of a finished product, without license, for subsequent sale. Recall the cases of Disney, Microsoft, and Lotus, taking Chinese pirates to court. Microsoft has lost millions and Disney saw video copies of *The Lion King* on Beijing streets before the video was even officially released there.

In 1992, then CIA director Robert Gates warned that nearly 20 foreign governments were carrying out economic intelligence gathering that was harmful to the interest of U.S. companies. Patrick Wilson, with the FBI, continues: "We're finding intelligence organizations from countries we've never looked at before who are active in the U.S." Former U.S. trade negotiator Michael B. Smith goes on to say that "other countries have active intelligence programs directed against our companies to give their companies a leg up."

The best way to identify espionage is to understand the form it generally takes. Robert Gates warns that foreign intelligence agencies of traditionally friendly countries "are trying to plant moles in American high-tech companies (and) search briefcases of American businessmen traveling overseas." Although it's a stereotype left over from the paranoia of the Cold War, the former Soviet Union was more successful than any other power in spying on Western industries. But the newer threats are less obvious ones. Now, even a U.S. Cold War ally such as France conducts organized surveillance of American companies. According to an anonymous source, "a secret CIA report recently warned of French agents roaming the U.S. looking for business secrets." And France has increased its intelligence budget steadily—even in the wake of the 1991 breakup of the Soviet Union. In 1992, the FBI delivered strong protests to France after

With expanding markets come new security challenges.

French Intelligence bumbled and was found to be operating against IBM and Texas Instruments.

Of course, the value of such intelligence operations for any government is unclear, especially when balanced against operating expenses and the political costs of potential discovery. But many countries simply don't buy the concept that their intelligence money might be better spent on education, R&D, or other areas that could help increase their competitiveness.

Terrorism is also an obvious threat to foreign business endeavors, and unfortunately, the new global economy offers plenty of targets for the media-savvy infidel. Evidence shows that terrorism has clearly moved beyond the scope of targeting military bases, county buildings, and World Trade Centers. According to the State Department, American executives were victims of more attacks in foreign countries in 1995 than all diplomatic or military personnel in all the U.S. embassies combined. As exporters rush into new, overseas markets, robberies, kidnappings, and other crimes against them have been climbing steadily. At the same times, downsizing and restructurings have hit security hard. Even the multinationals have been hit time and again—and they have their own security staffs to protect senior management abroad.

Surely, international security risks fluctuate with changing political events and regimes. However, security experts can point to areas that are likely to remain unstable and inhospitable climates for foreign business. Columbia and Peru are cited as the worst spots in South America due to the violence of drug cartels and the active presence of political terrorists. In Europe, Russia's organized criminals are known to prey on non-natives. In Africa, street crime is perilous in countries such as Kenya, South Africa, and Nigeria. In Asia, the rural areas of Pakistan and the Philippines are known for political violence and kidnappings. In Mexico, there have been reports of hooded gunmen stopping metered taxis on the street. The preferred victims are well-dressed businesspeople of either Latin or Caucasian descent. Similar situations exist around the globe, but because of more widespread foreign business activity and improved media and communications, it's now possible to more closely pinpoint high-crime areas. Although overblown media accounts have at times fueled public hysteria, the fact remains that kidnapping, robbery, and violence are legitimate concerns for those conducting business in foreign territory. Taking the necessary security precautions is simply one more step in the process of establishing your business for entry into the global marketplace.

Short of hiring its own security staff, the small business must learn to cope with such threats. Attacks against executives can generally be divided into two types: Those premeditated against them while at home; and those occasioned by a highly publicized visit.

There are three solid rules for maintaining your safety. The first is to stay inconspicuous in behavior and attire. Blend in with the scenery, eschewing tokens of the rich such as limos, fancy cars, private jets, Rolex watches, or other pieces of expensive jewelry. "Fly commercial and be sure to rent a car that is common at your destination site," says Christopher Marquet of Kroll Associates, one of the world's largest corporate security firms. Marquet offers other interesting tips, such as the fact that in Moscow, jeans are normal business attire. Wearing a suit would look out of place. And in some countries, be sure to wear contact lenses if required, as glasses are a sign of wealth.

As a second rule, identify trouble spots ahead of time. Optimally, an advance team would travel to and scout a particular site first, checking on airports, routes to hotels, and any place an executive might visit or pass through. Of course, this type of precautionary behavior may seem more suitable for a presidential visit than a business meeting, but there are times when it is necessary. Firms without the luxury or budget for such a deployment can call the regional security officer at the U.S. Embassy in the target country. Referrals and advice are available through the DOC (see the Appendix for a listing of contact information).

Third, anticipate potential attacks and implement preemptive safety measures. Company staffers should be strongly urged not to divulge the whereabouts of an envoy to callers or anyone making even the most informal of requests. They should not even divulge the fact that the executive is absent. The executive should also follow the same precautions. He or she should not give out travel information to those met during their journey. If propriety calls for it, be vague. In restaurants, seat yourself at tables in the back or away from windows. Avoid dining or jogging at the same place and time, and do not take the same route to appointments each day. Arrive at airports as close to departure time as possible, and wait in places beyond the major flow of travelers. Always remember that unpredictability is the best defense once you are abroad.

There are also special precautions for staying in hotels. The best security will be offered by internationally known hotels. Preferable are rooms above the first floor but below the eighth. They're less vulnerable to break-ins and easier to leave in the event of trouble. Also, do not let anyone into your room. If someone requests entry, call the front desk for authorization.

The importance of vigilance cannot be overstated. It should be exercised especially when entering or leaving your foreign destination. The executive who avoids unfamiliar areas is also a step ahead of attackers or surveillants who most commonly impersonate workaday types such a repairmen and street vendors.

As has been stressed throughout this book, what happens overseas often happens on U.S. shores as well. How many times have you read or heard of a businessperson being stopped on the street and persuaded to hand over his or her money? Perhaps we hear more about instances like these overseas than at home. Each year, millions of tourists depart the U.S. for destinations in the Far East, Latin America, Mexico, Europe, and elsewhere. There is absolutely no reason why your business experience abroad should be any less enjoyable, memorable, rewarding, and safe as it is for the vast majority of these travelers. Taking steps to better ensure your personal safety abroad involves a mixture of preliminary research and common sense—two things that certainly are not beyond the scope of the businessperson wishing to take part in the global economy!

We're at the relative dawn of an exciting age for business. The political, economic, and technological climates all point favorably to the expansion of business enterprises throughout the world. We've seen through this book that privatization, multicultural management, advanced communications technologies, and widespread use of the Internet are but a few of the trends that should facilitate foreign business endeavors in the years to come. And small businesses, because of their inherent flexibility and entrepreneurial spirit, are especially well-positioned to take advantage of the wealth of opportunities out there.

Be prepared for the rapid changes taking place on the global frontier by keeping your eyes and ears open for any and all changes occurring in your potential markets. While these emerging areas offer great opportunities for American businesses, you can limit your potential by ignoring the changing climates. By using this book as one of your resources for entering the global marketplace, it is our sincere hope that you'll feel armed with the knowledge that will make you better equipped to meet your global business goals.

Appendix

You may find yourself feeling as though you lack any useful tactical information at the onset of your sojourn into foreign business. This will quickly change once you begin investigating materials. In fact, you may find the sheer volume of material exceeds your capacity to process it.

The main problem is often where to look first. Oddly enough, some of the best sources are the last place most businesspeople would think to look for "authoritative" information. General business and tourist magazines are an excellent source for gleaning a variety of facts and opinions that will prove useful to getting you started on your search. For example, a magazine article on Brazilian beaches and nightlife may well disclose that Brazilians speak Portuguese, not Spanish. The same or another magazine may caution you that the work week ends on Thursday noon in Riyadh, Saudi Arabia; that in Germany, one does not offer a joke when making a speech; that the French prefer to entertain business guests at restaurants and clubs rather than at home; that only Americans commonly address each other by their first names; that a U.S. passport holder does not need a visa to enter Singapore, but does need one for Dubai; that the *Bangkok Post* is the leading English newspaper in Thailand; or that Chiang Kai-shek International Airport is located 25 miles from Taipei.

Other than magazines or travel brochures, you will find the following materials and services useful. Many are general resources, while some are more specific. Each will offer enough information to help you start your search. Most are inexpensive; some are free.

Business America. A biweekly magazine published regularly by the U.S. Department of Commerce provides a wealth of information related to foreign markets. Other countries and international associations also publish similar trade magazines. The list is too exhaustive to provide here, but a call to the DOC may yield the publication you are seeking.
(Call the DOC Hotline:
(800) USA-TRADE)

Commercial News U.S.A. is a noncommercial, magazine-style catalog published 10 times a year by the DOC. It is shipped to all the commercial sections of U.S. embassies and consulates, as well as to foreign subscribers. A U.S. manufacturer can place a listing with a photo and description of a single product for about $100 (a fraction of the cost of commercial advertising). Like all advertising, its message will attract potential buyers and may generate possible inquiries by distributors. The task of follow-up, however, will be yours.
(Call the DOC Hotline:
(800) USA-TRADE)

Training for Business Abroad

When conducting business abroad, an understanding of cultural differences and a knowledge of business customs, language, social, political, and economic institutions are crucial components of your success. There are programs and literature designed to enhance your ability to

cope and function in a new and foreign environment. Contact:
The International Society for Intercultural Education, Training, and Research (SIETAR International)
808 17th St., NW, Suite 200
Washington, D.C. 20006
(202) 466-7883
Offers information on programs of intercultural education, training, and research. Has a bimonthly newsletter/calendar of events, and a quarterly journal.

Intercultural Press
P.O. Box 700
Yarmouth, ME 04096
Write for an extensive list of titles on cross-cultural interaction. They also offer consultation services.

Embassies, consulates, and trade organizations. Almost all foreign embassies and consulates have a commercial section able to provide lists of trade publications and organizations within their countries. Typically, international trade associations themselves are extremely receptive to information requests. Examples of such organizations in the U.S. alone include the National Council of U.S. Exporters, the Trade Relations Council of the U.S., the Trade Information Center (TIC), DOC's International Trade Administration, the World Trade Center of New York, the World Trade Center of Chicago, the World Trade Center of Los Angeles, the California World Trade Commission (a state-run organization), and the Japanese External Trade Organization (JETRO).

To get an idea of what type of services trade organizations provide for businesses, we'll use JETRO as an example. JETRO arranges exhibitions and direct buyer-seller meetings, and handles public relations and promotions for exporters attempting to enter Japan. It also provides a data bank that summarizes products Japanese importers can tap into at any time. Other Japanese

sources include The Japanese Chamber of Commerce and Industry (U.S.- and Japan-based), the American Chamber of Commerce in Japan, and the Japan Export Information Center (JEIC). Of course Japan is just one example (albeit the world's second largest market) of a country in which to establish foreign business. Trade organizations exist for nearly every country actively pursuing trade with the U.S., and you can obtain contact information by looking in the "Government Pages" section in the front of your local phone book.

The transportation industry provides extensive information to would-be exporters. Why? Because it's clearly in their best interests to do so. Look to steamship lines, airlines, railways, trucking companies, long-distance phone companies, and package delivery firms for excellent and useful information.

Banks. Every major banking institution has an international department. Generally, the department publishes free booklets that help a new trader understand the sometimes arcane world of foreign credit, finance, and methods of payment.

Export Financing Assistance The Export-Import Bank (Eximbank) is an independent government agency with the primary purpose of facilitating the export of U.S. goods and services. Provides loans, guarantees, and insurance coverage to U.S. exporters and foreign buyers.
Contact: Export-Import Bank
Marketing and Program Division
811 Vermont Ave, NW
Washington, D.C. 20571
(800) 565-3946

Overseas Private Investment Corporation (OPIC) is a U.S. government agency that provides financing, insurance, and a variety of other investor services in more than 130 developing nations and emerging economies

throughout the world. Other investor services include: country and regional information, project and investor matching (via computer), advisory services, and outreach.
Contact: Overseas Private Investment Corporation
1100 New York Ave., NW
Washington, D.C. 20537

Department of Commerce. The DOC is your best source for information. It has nearly every tool and piece of information you'll need to go global, often even providing market surveys in specific markets for particular products. It administers its programs through 73 cities nationwide and maintains a list of certified and academic libraries. Approved sites house the DOC's trade database on CD-ROMs, containing research reports on 117 industries in 228 countries. The database is available by annual subscription at a starting rate of $150 for the single-user—on CD-ROM and over the Internet. But the database can also be accessed for free at one of the approved federal depository libraries. DOC specialists also provide guide sheets on particularly thorny export problems, such as qualifying for the low tariffs now available under NAFTA. General consultations and information are free.
Department of Commerce Hotline:
(800) USA-TRADE
DOC District Office Listings:
(202) 377-2000
Internet Listing:
http://www.stat-usa.gov

Export Mailing Lists. Also known as export contact lists or the Foreign Trade Index (FTI). To use this service, you need to contact a DOC district office for your product's Harmonized Tariff Schedule Classification (HTSC). Once obtained, the DOC office will provide a list of names and addresses of companies located in a given country that are importing products similar to your own. The cost is $.25 per name.
Contact: (202) 377-2000

Trade Fairs and Exhibitions
Each year, the Commerce Department and the private sector (under the Commerce department certification program) schedule about 80 international trade fairs and exhibitions around the world. In addition to the enhanced exposure of their product or service, participants get pre- and post-event logistical and transportation support, and extensive overseas marketing and promotional campaigns.
Contact: Trade Information Center
(800) 872-8723

Matchmaker Trade Delegations
As described in Chapter 1, these delegations, organized and led by DOC personnel, enable firms new to global business to meet pre-screened prospects who are interested in selling their product or services in overseas markets. The trips typically last a week or less and target major markets in two countries. Thorough briefings on market requirements and business practices and interpreters' services are provided. Delegation members pay their own expenses.
Contact: Export Promotion Services
International Trade Administration
(202) 482-4457

Small Business Development Centers Funded jointly by the SBA and private agencies, SBDCs also provide support for businesses contemplating international trade. Services include: assistance with joint ventures and licensing programs; packaging international trade finance loans; language training and translation services; and help with overseas trade shows.
Contact: Association of Small Business Development Centers
1313 Farnam St., Suite 132
Omaha, NE 68182
(402) 595-2387

Export Opportunity Hotline. The Hotline is sponsored by the Small Business Administration (SBA), a nonprofit organization based in Washington, D.C. Because the SBA's focus is the small-business person, it may provide especially useful information to the business with a limited staff and budget. The SBA fields experts on finding foreign distributors, cheap ways to test products overseas, and tips on further market research. Businesses going global can also get advice on solving problems they've encountered. This service is free.
Contact: (800) 243-7232
(in Washington, D.C.): (202) 223-1104

Service Corps of Retired Executives. SCORE works in conjunction with the Small Business Administration, offering the expertise of retired executives for your business problems. These business veterans are known for providing assistance to exporters, especially in the field of strategy. SCORE has 370 chapters and roughly 500 counselors throughout the U.S.
Contact: (800) 634-0245

Export Legal Assistance Network. A law firm with international exper-

tise is a good starting point for many global businesses. Network advice is available on anything from protecting patents and trademarks to drafting contracts with new partners. The network provides free referrals to local attorneys with trade experience. Member attorneys will provide one free counseling session for new exporters. The program is administered through the DOC. The network's national coordinator is Judd L. Kessler, at the law firm of Porter, Wright, Morris & Arthur, in Washington, D.C.
DOC Contact: (800) USA-TRADE
Judd L. Kessler: (202) 778-3000

International Standards Organization. The ISO represents 91 countries that have collectively set general worldwide manufacturing standards. Companies wishing to do the widest possible business abroad should have their operations certified by an ISO-accredited examiner. The American Society for Quality Control can help put companies in touch with such examiners. It also connects callers with other companies that have gone through the process.
Contact: (800) 248-1946

Glossary

A

Advance against documents A loan made on the security of documents covering the shipment.

Advising bank A bank, operating in the exporter's country, which handles letters of credit for a foreign bank by notifying the export firm that the credit has been opened in its favor. The advising bank fully informs the exporter of the conditions to the letter of credit without necessarily bearing responsibility for payment.

Aftermarket service Servicing a product after its sale. For overseas sales, aftermarket service requires maintaining an adequate sales staff that is able to understand English service manuals and make repairs to the product. It also requires stocking spare parts and flying personnel stateside or to training centers to attend classes.

Agent Distributor Service (ADS) Arguably the best service the DOC offers small businesses poised to go global. An attaché at any one of the DOC's 107 foreign offices will distribute a U.S. company's product catalog to local parties thought to have any interest in representing or buying the product line. As responses are received, the DOC attaché will compile a list of interested parties for the U.S. company.

Air waybill A bill of lading that covers both domestic and international flights transporting goods to a specific destination. This is a non-negotiable instrument of air transport that serves as a receipt for the shipper, in that the carrier has accepted the goods listed and obliges itself to carry the consignment to the airport of destination according to specific conditions.

American Depository Receipt A receipt issued by a stateside depository bank holding a number of securities of foreign companies that correspond to the receipts. Such receipts can trade on American exchanges just as domestic stock is traded.

B

Brand loyalty The surest and fastest way to achieve long-term marketing success. Marketing theories hold that products with established brand names will perform better and outlast similar products without the benefit of name recognition. Typically, brand loyalty is often built through expensive marketing and promotional blitzes.

C

Certificate of inspection A document certifying that merchandise (such as perishable goods) was in good condition immediately prior to its shipment.

Certificate of manufacture A statement (often notarized) in which a producer of goods certifies that manufacture has been completed and that the goods are now at the disposal of the buyer.

Certificate of origin A document required by certain foreign countries for tariff purposes, certifying the country origin of specified goods.

Commission agents Scouts for overseas buyers, they act as middlemen between foreign buyers and U.S. manufacturers. Paid purely on commission when and if a product or service is sold.

Contract manufacturing An agreement whereby a foreign company undertakes to manufacture a product on behalf of a U.S. company. The product is to be made according to specifications and quality guidelines provided by the U.S. company. Typical to the arrangement is a transfer of technology and company secrets. Natural or forced closure of the agreement will often result in the spawning of a new competitor from a one-time partner.

Correspondent bank A bank that, in its own country, handles the business of a foreign bank.

Counterfeiters Thieves of intellectual property who duplicate it and package it for sale as the original. Entertainment-related concerns and software manufacturers are particularly hard hit by counterfeiters.

Countertrade The sale of goods or services that are paid whole or in part by the transfer of goods or services in a foreign country.

Cyber cash A means of enabling direct cash transactions over the Internet. The digitizing of money.

Demographics The size, density, growth, and distribution of the human population within certain markets. Studied to determine the suitability of a product therein.

Department of Commerce (DOC) The U.S. Department of Commerce promotes the nation's international trade. It offers assistance and information to U.S. businesses and potential overseas partners in an effort to up American competitiveness in the global economy.

Through 73 district offices in the U.S. and 107 countries worldwide, the DOC's primary functions are to introduce American-made products to foreign markets, prevent unfair foreign competition, provide social and economic statistics and analyses, provide research and support for the increased use of scientific and technological development, grant patents and registered trademarks, develop policies and conducting research on telecommunications and the telecommunications industry, provide assistance to promote domestic economic development, promote travel to the U.S. by residents of foreign countries, and assist in the growth of minority businesses. The DOC's main office is located at Fourteenth Street between Constitution Avenue and E Street NW, Washington, D.C. 20230. The phone number is (202) 482-2000. Or they are available through their Web site: http://www.trade

Direct distribution A means of moving a company's products overseas. Considered to be fast and efficient, though more expensive than passive distribution. Involves face-to-face meetings with prospective distributors abroad. The foreign rep is then charged with the responsibility of pushing the company's product, usually in a specified market and over a given period of time.

Distributorships An individual or firm specifically contracted to represent a manufacturer's product in specific territories. Hiring distributors is the most widely used method of entry into foreign trade. Often less capital intensive than other methods of entry. Used a step or two prior to a firm opening an overseas subsidiary.

Downsizing The making smaller of a company or a subsidiary therein; motivated by a perceived need to restore life to the ailing and noncompetitive entity. Proponents espouse that downsizing increases competitiveness, allowing for expansion and rehirings in the future from a better, more educated labor force. Opponents perceive downsizing as a heartless corporate move creating the commoditization of human labor.

Draft An unconditional order in writing from one person (the drawer) to another (the drawee), directing the drawee to pay a specified amount to a named drawer at a fixed or determinable future date.

Drawback Articles manufactured or produced in the United States with the use of imported components or raw materials and exported are entitled to a refund of up to 99 percent duty charged on the imported components. The refund is known as a drawback.

Economic unity Governments overlooking political and ideological differences in favor of shared economic goals.

Emerging economy A developing nation's economy that is poised to grow.

Encryption Software technology in place and under development that will help make cash transactions over the Internet secure. Fundamentally, encryption treats cash as digitized units and assigns private and pubic digital "keys" to the buyer and seller. Transactions are conducted by both parties using these keys to send and retrieve payment.

European Monetary Union (EMU) The EMU is made up of 15 member countries as listed below in "European Union." The EMU is undertaking to end the political management of major currencies in Europe. A single currency is being sought, called the "Euro," though will be possible only once at least four EU countries have imple-

mented mutually fixed exchange rates between their own currencies and the Euro. The deadline is May 30th, 2001. Furthermore, membership in the EMU requires that a country's deficit cannot exceed the rigid standard of 3 percent of its GDP by 2000. This has several countries scrambling, as current European deficits are running at about 4.5 percent of GDP. Information pertaining to the EMU's progress is posted regularly on the Web site: http://www.euronet.nl

European Union (EU) The EU is made up of 15 member states including Austria, Belgium, Denmark, Finland, France, Germany, Greece, Ireland, Italy, Luxembourg, The Netherlands, Portugal, Spain, Sweden, and the United Kingdom. The principal aim of the EU is to promote balanced and sustainable economic progress by opening borders and forging closer unions between the peoples of the 15 countries and their cultures. A single monetary unit, the "Euro," has been proposed as has a common defense policy. The business of the EU and its ministers is posted regularly on its Web site: http://www.europa

Exclusive distribution Granting to an overseas distributor exclusive rights to represent a product in a specified territory. U.S. companies are sometimes known overseas for playing "lean and mean." That is, giving the distribution of their products to more than one distributor, sometimes unbeknownst to all the players.

Eximbank Export-Import Bank of the United States.

Expatriates Non-native residents in a foreign country.

Export-Import Bank The U.S. Export-Import Bank is a government agency that assists in the export financing of U.S. goods and services through a variety of loans, loan guarantees to commercial lenders, and insurance programs for qualifying exporters. It is particularly helpful to small businesses seeking aid in taking their products to the global marketplace. Briefing programs are also offered to the small business community around the country. The Eximbank has a special U.S. toll-free number, (800) 565-EXIM, or can be reached on the Internet at http://www.exim.gov

Export Management Company EMCs function as the supplier's or manufacturer's export department (manufacturer reps are their domestic counterparts). They take on all the functions of an in-house staff, such as appointing foreign distributors, managing a manufacturer's sales and marketing efforts, handling shipping and export documentation, collecting payments, etc.

Forced commoditization Taking a novel idea and mass producing it.

Former Soviet Bloc countries The 15 constituent republics that were once a part of the Soviet Union.

Free-trade zone A port designated by the government of a country for duty-free entry on any nonprohibited goods. Merchandise may be stored, displayed, used for manufacturing, etc., in the zone and reexported without duties being paid. Duties are imposed on the merchandise (or items manufactured from the merchandise) only when the goods pass from the zone into the area of the country subject to customs authority.

General Agreement on Tariffs and Trade (GATT) GATT is a multilateral treaty much like NAFTA. It has since been replaced, in January 1995, by the World Trade Organization.

Initially, GATT was intended to help reduce trade barriers between signatory countries and to promote trade through tariff concessions. Conditions within the treaty were intended to favor developing countries, particularly by encouraging industrial countries to assist the trade of those less-developed nations.

Global expansion Taking business operations worldwide.

Global Village A term coined by trend forecaster Marshall McKuhan over 30 years ago. Refers to open borders between countries for the free trade of goods and services.

Going Global The act of creating overseas markets for a domestically produced product.

Gold Key Program Sponsored by the DOC. Arranges for small-business executives to meet with pre-screened potential partners in foreign countries—often at U.S. embassies there.

Hidden fees Discretionary fees levied by governments in the form of taxes, tariffs, or other fees.

Hot spots Countries, or territories within, where there is a sudden explosion of growth across the economy or in a particular industry. Typically driving the growth are political reforms meant to cut red tape and to induce free-market experimentation.

Information Superhighway See Internet.

Infrastructure Includes structures and emplacements necessary to conduct adequate business telecommunications besides the traditional definition of roads, navigable waterways, and a distribution system for power.

Intellectual property Creative property often in the form of movies, books, music, or software that can be copyrighted, but that often suffers overseas from cheap and easy counterfeiting.

International Monetary Fund (IMF) The IMF was created in 1944 and now has a membership roster that includes 181 countries. Foremost, it is known for its large cash reserve from which it offers financial assistance to qualifying member countries. Other purposes the IMF has undertaken are: promoting international monetary cooperation; facilitating the growth of international trade; promoting exchange stability; assisting in the establishment of a multilateral system of payments; making the general resources of the fund temporarily available to member countries under adequate safeguards, as mentioned; and doing away with the disequilibrium in the international balances of payment by member countries. The IMF can be contacted in the U.S. at External Relations Department, International Monetary Fund, Washington, D.C. 20431. Its phone is (202) 623-7300. Or it can be contacted through its Web site: http://www.imf.org

Internet Primarily a medium of free information exchange over telephone lines. Lately, businesses are viewing it as a freeway to markets. A few computers scattered around the globe control the Internet, and anyone with a computer, a modem, and the appropriate software can tap into it. The Internet grew out of a Defense Department program intended to link remote computers for weapons development, research, and other military uses. When the military abandoned it, university and scientific communities jumped in and continued to develop what we have since termed the "Internet."

ISO 9000 Certificate The International Standards Organization is a federation of 91 countries that have set a generalized series of quality systems, standards, and guidelines that certify the consistency of the way a company produces and delivers its products and services. ISO-certified examiners certifying a company require that all aspects of manufacturing, safety, and quality control be universally standardized. Companies not qualifying will likely be turned away from doing business in member nations. Information offered on courses pertaining to ISO 9000 standards can be obtained on the Internet at: http://www.np.ac.sg.~hsl/iso.htm

Letter of credit (L/C) A document, issued by the bank per the instructions by a buyer of goods, authorizing the seller to draw a specified sum of money under specified terms.

Licensing agreement A low-cost method of entry into a foreign marketplace. Deemed the optimal arrangement for smaller manufacturers wishing to enter a foreign marketplace in which tariffs and duties are too high to ship directly or when a lack of infrastructure creates freight and shipping barriers. Under a licensing agreement with a foreign company, royalties are paid back to the exporter. Inherent in the relationship, though, is a transfer of technology, knowledge, company secrets, and possibly intellectual property.

Link-ups People continents away interacting via video as though face-to-face.

Local markets Markets defined by territory rather than products. On a global scale, local markets may consist of an entire country, countries, or some designated area within.

M

Market research Undertaking to study every applicable law, political philosophy, and business condition that may affect a product and the marketing of it, including any cultural, social, or economic trend or factor that could be relevant in the short or long run of the product's life. Market surveys should investigate whether a market exists for a particular product in the target area, what uncontrollable factors might be encountered on entering the market, and what aspects of the market can be controlled to help maximize returns.

MITU "Made in the USA." Trade shows promoted by the DOC. MITU shows travel monthly to new countries and cover more than one industry. For a fee, products can be included. The manufacturer need not be present.

Matchmakers Sponsored by local DOC offices. A trade delegation of top U.S. executives that arranges meetings, factory visits, symposia, and even dinner banquets. Somewhat expensive, but high profile and surrounded by big business contacts.

Mother Goose Company Companies that piggyback other products on top of their own.

Multicultural management The use of ethnically diverse managers in operations around the world for the purpose of bridging cultural gaps, better integrating a company and its products into the market, and achieving a greater understanding of overall and ongoing market conditions.

N

National Small Business United NSBU has been an advocate for small business since it was founded in 1937. With 65,000 U.S. members, it is a lobbying force that works closely with the House of Representatives and the Senate in efforts to promote small-business interests and address member concerns. NSBU maintains several chapters and affiliate organizations across the U.S. Information can be obtained from the main office at: National Small Business United, 1156 15th Street, NW, Suite 1100, Washington, D.C. 20005. The phone is (202) 872-8543. The E-mail address is: nsbu@nsbu.org The Web site address is: http://www.nsbu.org

National Trade Data Bank Information compiled by the government that has been distilled into the form of trade leads and market research reports. Further information is available through their Web site: http://www.stat-usa.gov

Native companies Companies based in a particular country and staffed by natives of that country.

North American Free Trade Agreement (NAFTA) NAFTA is the high profile, low-tariff pact and trading bloc treaty signed by the U.S., Canada, and Mexico in 1993. Each year North American tariffs are being lowered in conjunction with the agreement.

Outsourcing Forging agreements with foreign manufacturers to produce products that on completion are to be shipped back to the U.S. company or to a destination specified by it. Lower wages paid to native workers is often seen as a chief benefit of outsourcing.

Pacific Rim The countries aligned along the Western shores of the Pacific or seas adjoining it; principally Japan, Australia, New Zealand, the

South Pacific Islands, Cambodia, Hong Kong, Indonesia, China, South Korea, Laos, Macao, Malaysia, Myanmar, New Zealand, the Philippines, Singapore, Taiwan, Thailand, and South Vietnam.

Pacific Tiger countries Emerging economies along the Pacific Rim, notably Hong Kong, Singapore, Taiwan, China, Indonesia, Malaysia, and the Philippines.

Passive distribution Closely related to passive marketing. Low up-front costs, but consequences are that it is often ineffective. Typically, an entity or individual usually unknown to the manufacturer undertakes to distribute its product. Other drawbacks include difficulty in forecasting product demand shifts or lack of interest entirely, the risk of a distributor being powerless to move a product, and the presence of middlemen, among other factors. Generally, passive distribution is regarded as short-sighted over the long haul in global trade because it does not qualify as a means of international marketing.

Piggyback companies Act as carriers of products that are not competitive with their own. Such will ship other products with their own, making up a package that it deems attractive. Drawbacks are that this is not a form of marketing and any piggybacked product will suffer from lack of name recognition, on which success is often built.

Piracy Theft of property—typically, theft of intellectual property.

Privatizations The selling-off of state assets. Undertaken to raise cash and slash budget deficits. Generally, for larger companies, equity sales are divided into lots, and only so much of a company is sold off in any one year. Privatizations are particularly popular in European and Latin American countries. Financing most of the trend is American money.

Protectionism The practice of imposing tariffs on exporters to protect domestic products and companies.

Provincialism For countries and government, the act of limiting economic perspective to its own borders only.

Public-key cryptography See Encryption. The mechanical/digital process of conducting an exchange of cash over the Internet. Each party in a transaction holds two software "keys." Public keys are published while private keys are known only to their holder. Both keys are needed to encode and decode a message that contains the digital equivalent of cash. Note that public-key cryptography is not limited to cyber cash only. It can also be used for the safe and confidential passage of closely held information.

Punitive tariffs Taxes on imported goods meant to punish the exporter for policies detrimental to the country where the goods and/or services are landed.

Sell-offs The sale of assets or subsidiaries, usually from privately run and owned companies.

Shareholder activists Usually investors wishing to rid companies of entrenched, unproductive management. Activists may also commonly press issues that will make a company more competitive, increase profits, or streamline operations.

Small Business Development Centers (SBDC) Administered by the U.S. Small Business Administration (SBA). SBDC branch locations are housed at various universities around the country in all 50 states and in the District of Columbia, Puerto Rico, and the Virgin Islands. At these subcenters, experts from professional and trade associations including the legal and banking community, academia, the chamber of commerce, and SCORE (the Service Corps of Retired Executives) provide management assistance to present and prospective small business owners. Principal aims are to deliver counseling, training and technical assistance in all aspects of small business management including international trade. For the nearest SBDC subcenter, call the Small Business Answer Desk at 1-800-8-ASK-SBA or (202) 205-7064. Information can also be accessed through the SBDC's Web site: http://www.nttc.edu/assist/sbdc.html

Soft trader Sellers of computer software and entertainment-related media formats.

Soft products Software and intellectual properties.

State assets Often monopolies that are owned by the state.

Subdistribution Distribution conducted at a level below primary distribution. Usually conducted by a person or company contracted by the primary distributor.

Tariffs Duties imposed by a government on imported and/or exported goods.

Trade Shows/Missions Convention-type shows sponsored by the DOC on a regular basis. Provide networking opportunities on the exhibit floor where booths are rented and from which products are examined by buyers or distributors.

Trading blocs Two or more countries forming a pact whereby a business registering its products in one of the countries is tantamount to registration in any other member country.

Value-added Tax (VAT) Taxes levied by countries on imported parts that the government perceives as adding value to an existing product. These taxes are over and above any tariffs, duties or import taxes already imposed on the import.

W

World Bank Formally known as the International Bank for Reconstruction and Development. Known as a "lender of last resort" as it makes loans to developing countries that have a minimum level of creditworthiness. Interest rates are low and loan maturity periods are generous. But it is expected that as a borrowing country's per capita income increases, it will "graduate" and stop borrowing from the World Bank. Over its 50-year history, the World Bank has lent $277 billion to developing countries and economic institutions. Loan money is typically raised on world financial markets. For more information, contact The World Bank Group, Business Partnership Center, 1818 H Street, NW, Washington, D.C. 20433. The phone number is (202) 522-4272. E-mail is received at: business partner@worldbank.org The Web site is at: http://www.worldbank.org

World Trade Organization (WTO) The WTO is the successor to GATT. As provided by the WTO, it is "the legal and institutional foundation for the multilateral trading system. It provides the principal contractual obligations determining how governments frame and implement domestic trade legislation and regulations. And it is the platform on which trade relations among countries evolve through collective debate, negotiation and adjudication." Principally, WTO member countries are seeking to reduce tariffs and other trade barriers and to nullify any discriminatory treatment sometimes present in international trade relations. Information is available at: World Trade Organization, Centre William Rappard, 154, rue de Lausanne, CH-1211 Geneva, Switzerland. Or the WTO can be contacted by phone by following international calling instructions combined with the number, 7395111.

The Web site is: http://www.wto.org

World Wide Web Sites on the Internet that hold information pertinent to a product, place or business. With the right software and computer accessories, anyone can design and install a site. Some sites can be used free-of-charge, while others charge access fees.

Index